LEARNING TO CHANGE THE WORLD

LEARNING TO CHANGE THE WORLD

THE SOCIAL IMPACT OF ONE LAPTOP PER CHILD

WALTER BENDER, CHARLES KANE, JODY CORNISH, AND NEAL DONAHUE

palgrave
macmillan

KH

LEARNING TO CHANGE THE WORLD
Copyright © Walter Bender, Charles Kane, Jody Cornish, and Neal Donahue,
2012.

First published in 2012 by PALGRAVE MACMILLAN® in the U.S.—a division
of St. Martin's Press LLC, 175 Fifth Avenue, New York, NY 10010.

Where this book is distributed in the UK, Europe and the rest of the world, this
is by Palgrave Macmillan, a division of Macmillan Publishers Limited, registered
in England, company number 785998, of Houndmills, Basingstoke, Hampshire
RG21 6XS.

Palgrave Macmillan is the global academic imprint of the above companies and
has companies and representatives throughout the world.

Palgrave® and Macmillan® are registered trademarks in the United States, the
United Kingdom, Europe and other countries.

ISBN: 978-0-230-33731-2

Library of Congress Cataloging-in-Publication Data is available from the
Library of Congress.

A catalogue record of the book is available from the British Library.

Design by Letra Libre

First edition: December 2012

10 9 8 7 6 5 4 3 2 1

Printed in the United States of America.

10/6/14

CONTENTS

Five pages of photographs appear between pages 102 and 103.

All proceeds from sales of the book go directly to
One Laptop per Child and Sugar Labs.

THE VIEW FROM THE INSIDE

IN THE WORDS OF WALTER BENDER AND CHARLES KANE

I OFTEN ASK ENGINEERS TO DESCRIBE A GREAT LEARNING MO-ment in their lives. Inevitably, they describe wrestling with a difficult problem that they were passionate about: making many false starts, consulting with colleagues, scouring the Internet for ideas, and eventually coming up with a workable solution. I then ask a follow-up question: How would you use technology in the classroom? Immediately they revert to their own classroom experience and just as inevitably reinvent the worksheet in a computerized form. No one has ever answered my first question about a great learning moment by saying "Taking a multiple-choice test" or "Listening to a lecture." Yet when they design technology for learning, they revert to a passive model in which the student is receiving information rather than designing a technology to enable students to rapidly prototype ideas, explore, and collaborate. They *know* what great learning looks and feels like, but they *believe* that school is about instructing. Reconciling what we know with what we believe remains the great challenge for school reform and the day-to-day challenge faced by One Laptop per Child (OLPC) in its attempt to change the way we educate the children of the world. It is also the challenge faced by social entrepreneurs, who want to do what they *know* is of social value within the context of a business climate that *believes* in the status quo.

If you are among those who think that OLPC was "just about the laptop," you are not alone; it is a common misconception. It is important to state, though, that OLPC's mission was never simply to build the

$100 laptop—although that accomplishment alone is worth celebrating. Our goal was to enable a global paradigm shift in the way in which we help children learn. It was about giving children tools that would empower them by teaching them to think, explore, innovate, and create. In the context of developing world social and economic realities, where access to knowledge and opportunity are so constrained, teaching children these critical skills can make a tangible difference in their life trajectory and that of their families. In our emerging global reality, giving children the tools of innovation and critical thinking is vital in enabling them to address the legacy of complex and seemingly intractable problems past generations have created for them.

As you will learn in this book, we didn't think of everything and we didn't get everything right. Building the laptop was not an overnight decision. The approach we took has its roots in decades of research at MIT and reflects deliberate decisions to approach education in a new way in order to change, over time, the culture of school. This book is about much more than "the $100 laptop." It is about the work that OLPC has engaged in to try to revolutionize education and make it accessible to all children, regardless of their social and economic circumstances. The $100 laptop—also known as the XO laptop—was a tool that we created to enable a new approach to education.[1]

OLPC emerged from the work of the MIT Media Lab, a research group that we founded in MIT's Architecture School in 1985. Our mission at the Media Lab was to "invent a better future" through development of tools that promote human adaptability. At MIT and in the Media Lab, a number of strands of thinking from technology, design, multimedia, and education came together in a new and interesting way.

A primary influence was the work of pioneering computer scientist Alan Kay, who coined the term "personal computer" in the early 1970s. In Kay's view, computers enhance five things: (1) getting and holding our attention, (2) word processing, (3) information retrieval, (4) simulation, and (5) interpersonal communication. By fortuitous coincidence, my research group at the Media Lab was adjacent to the Epistemology[2] and Learning Group led by Seymour Papert, a revolutionary thinker in education. Seymour explored how to help students to learn in ways that give them not just knowledge, but skills. When he came to MIT in the mid-1960s, Papert brought with him the insight that a computer could be "a thing to think with."

Through my work with Kay, Papert, and others, I realized there was one more item to add to Kay's list of what computers enable for people: learning. The "construction" of knowledge is potentially more important than acquisition of new knowledge. We would say that building new skills through a well-designed process of learning is, in fact, the point of education. Given the opportunity to be expressive and exploratory in the learning process, learners—and in particular young learners—can master powerful ideas and gain not simply new knowledge, but new skills. This is true even when (in contrast with what happens at MIT) they are learning outside, under a tree, in a remote part of an impoverished country.

Where I had previously focused on creating tools for personalized *consumption* of media, such as a personalized newspaper or television news, I now began to explore how to enable users to *create*—for example by writing, editing, illustrating, and redesigning their own publications. One of my graduate students, Mark Kortegaas, developed a system whereby students could combine wire-service news with their own writing. Seeing fifth graders doing what later would be called "blogging" convinced me that the real power of computing was in reestablishing a balance between consumers and creators.[3] With even very modest tools, we could enable an unprecedented level of engagement, activism, and learning.

In 1985, my students and I got involved in Papert's one-to-one computing pilot at the Hennigan School, a public elementary school in the Jamaica Plain neighborhood of Boston. The project, called "Children as Software Designers," engaged elementary students in making their own piece of software over the course of two to three months. In creating software, children really had to become both teachers and programmers, able to understand and communicate the ideas and how things work. Through this process they learned more than they would have by using pre-existing software. Over the next twenty years, I had frequent collaboration with Papert and his students, working with teachers and learners from Boston to Bangkok and revisiting the theme of "learning through doing" again and again, with the computer as the medium for exploration.[4]

One Laptop per Child emerged as a direct follow-on to our work with Papert. In my thirty years at MIT, six years as Executive Director of the MIT Media Lab, and now as founder of Sugar Labs—an organization that focuses on ongoing development of the software for the XO—my personal focus is giving children the tools they need to make learning happen, even in absence of an effective, formalized school experience. In our approach, we do not emphasize classroom tools or codifying a specific curriculum or body of knowledge. Our focus is on informal time with the computer, since, as MIT Professor Marvin Minsky observed, "the playfulness of childhood is the most demanding teacher we will ever have."[5] By creating a laptop with content and software designed specifically for children, we felt that we could bring a better educational experience to children that would enable collaborative, self-empowered learning. By making the laptop low-cost, low-power, and connected, we could make this experience available to even the world's poorest children. As we observed over thirty years, when children have access to this type of tool, they get engaged in their own learning: they share, create, and collaborate. "They become connected to each other, to the world, and to a brighter future."

Antonio Battro, a specialist in cognitive and perceptual development and Education Officer for OLPC, used to say that "everyone is both a teacher and learner."[6] With this book, we hope both to do some teaching about OLPC and to create a foundation for mutual learning regarding education, technology, and social entrepreneurship. We hope that the book will challenge some of the common—and we think limited—conceptions about both the potential of children and, in the process, dispel some of the common misunderstandings of OLPC. We also hope that the book will inspire you to contribute to our efforts, both by supporting specific initiatives that OLPC is driving and by becoming engaged and involved in changing the approach to education being taken globally. Finally, we hope that this book will enable other social entrepreneurs attempting bold social change to learn both from our mistakes and our successes.

—*Walter Bender*
Founder of Sugar Labs, cofounder of OLPC, and former
Executive Director of the MIT Media Lab

I HAVE A SHORTER HISTORY WITH ONE LAPTOP PER CHILD (OLPC) than my coauthor. I joined the organization in the latter half of 2006, at the point at which the basic design for the XO laptop was solidified and we were beginning to explore potential partnerships. As I came to OLPC with more than twenty years of experience as CEO and CFO of a number of hardware and software technology companies, I was an outlier, to say the least, among the staff of MIT computer scientists and educators. Before meeting Nicholas Negroponte, I had never heard of OLPC. In speaking with him, however, it took only a matter of minutes for me to appreciate the scope of social impact that the OLPC project could achieve. I was hooked. Excited to take on a noble cause and daunting challenge with potential to scale globally, I signed on to serve as CFO for the salary of zero dollars.

When I joined OLPC, I came with the understanding that the laptop would sell for $100; after all, every article referring to OLPC talks about the "$100 laptop." And I assumed there would be a small margin between cost of production and this $100 price tag. When I asked about real cost of production, the response was that costs would approach $200 per computer. Red flag. My second question was about the support and implementation capabilities that were in place once the laptops were shipped to users. The response was, "Not sure, since we don't have people to do that." Hmmm. This clearly was not going to be the business model to which I was accustomed. In fact, the supply chain management and associated financial requirements were going to be unique in many ways.

What became abundantly clear was the need for real business discipline to assert itself for OLPC to be successful in its production and distribution phases. The key challenge on the horizon was how to build the financial and organizational foundation to manufacture and deliver millions of machines. For any entrepreneurial endeavor, this point— where the clarity of the idea or mission meets the realities of defining a service model and preparing to deliver at scale—is a real test of an organization's ability to adapt and learn.

As it became apparent that the challenges were far more than financial, my role at OLPC quickly evolved to president and chief operating officer. I came to understand that many of the decisions OLPC had made in pursuit of its goal to radically empower learning for kids also upended traditional business models for design, manufacture, distribution, and support of technology.

Through a combination of internal and external developments, we found ourselves in the difficult and unprecedented position of managing sales, hardware and software development, manufacturing, and product support. For those who know the technology industry, there are entire industry sectors, comprising multiple Fortune 500 companies devoted to each of these activities. At the point where I joined, OLPC was an organization of less than twenty full-time staff, composed of primarily engineers and a skeleton crew of support staff. For OLPC to achieve scale, new models of collaboration and coordination would need to be developed and proven. We had a choice: innovate or fail, not just with our technology, but also with our financial model.

OLPC did not set out to manufacture computers. In fact, Nicholas Negroponte and I spent a great deal of time and effort trying to convince larger computer manufacturers to build and brand the machine. The barrier for these firms was how to integrate a non-profit venture into their for-profit business model. We were ultimately unsuccessful in forging partnerships with these firms (although we would argue that we played a real role in convincing these companies to enter the emerging low-cost "netbook" market). Instead, we continued to work directly with multiple manufacturing and distribution partners—including Quanta, Brightstar, AMD, and Chi Mei—to build and deliver laptops.

Our supply chain approach created real constraints for sales and customer relationship. Needing to closely manage production costs and lacking the depth of an organization to support multiple small orders, we had to aim for high-volume orders of 100,000 or more. Selling first-generation computers, sight unseen, is difficult in and of itself, let alone doing so at high volume. We had to rely on purchasers, primarily governments, to establish their own infrastructure and delivery capability once the computers arrived in country. Contrary to most technology companies, which charge as much as 20 percent of the original price as a yearly maintenance fee, we charged no maintenance fee because we did not plan to support the computers in country. To solve the problem of spare parts, we shipped an additional 1 percent of the original order to provide excess machines to backfill in case of broken machines or required spare parts.

I often quipped with Nicholas Negroponte that the risks he took to get the project off the ground in the early stages defied strict business logic of risk and related return. His design was radical and groundbreaking, the development approach was risky and unproven, and the public pronouncements made about goals and impact were bold, to say the least. Looking back, I am glad I was not around in the early stages, as I am certain I would have challenged some or all of these choices and, in so doing, business logic would have weakened OLPC's potential in the early stages of the project.

One of my personal learnings from this project is the importance of balancing risk taking and business discipline. Business is not a bad word when it comes to non-profits. So often, people working in the non-profit sector think of "businessmen" as too rigid and lacking in creativity and commitment to the greater good. Increasingly, however, it's clear that bringing together a strong social mission with rigorous business discipline can be a powerful force for positive change. Under a non-profit umbrella, greater risks are possible, which creates the possibility for greater innovation. For social entrepreneurs who can bring a clear sense of mission, an innovative vision and approach, and business knowledge and discipline, the opportunities for impact are astounding.

I have traveled all over the world to do presentations about OLPC to universities and business schools, both to tell the OLPC story and to recruit support for our work. What strikes me most from these presentations is how engaged this new generation of students is compared to my "boomer" generation. They are bursting with energy and desire to make a difference in the world, for the sake of the impact rather than purely for the money. It is this continued interest that keeps our project alive and growing. My sincere hope is that this book serves as an ongoing reminder that the talents of these young people can be utilized to vastly improve the world. I also hope that the story of building OLPC can serve as guidance for others struggling with the challenges of building a social enterprise on a global scale.

For all readers of this book, I hope that you will pause and reflect on the look in the eyes of a child using the XO. This child has so very little, but is eager to learn and do so much. The reward for your involvement in this great project becomes so evident.

—Charles Kane
Board of Directors, OLPC Association; Senior Lecturer,
Finance, MIT Sloan Graduate School of Management;
Former President and Chief Operating Officer, OLPC

ON THE OUTSIDE, LOOKING IN

A WORD FROM JODY CORNISH AND NEAL DONAHUE

T HE IDEA TO WORK ON THIS BOOK WITH WALTER AND Chuck came from our prior, shared conviction that One Laptop per Child—as a concept and as an organization—might have missed the boat. OLPC is enormously well-known across the education, technology, and social-change sectors—perhaps matched only by such giants as Habitat for Humanity, Greenpeace, and Teach for America in name recognition—and the $100 laptop is a widely recognized reference. In our work in international development and US-focused social change, we would encounter mention of OLPC time and again, and often with a significant amount of negative emotion and criticisms attached. It seemed to us that there was a fundamental mismatch between the amount of attention and recognition the organization had received, and our view—from the outside looking in—of the faulty and inconsistent logic that underpinned its approach to revolutionizing education in the developing world.

After assisting in editing the first case study on OLPC used for an international case competition held by the Hult International School of Business in 2010, we were even more intrigued: OLPC clearly was struggling to bring fully into focus its approach to its next phase of growth and to address some of the pointed criticisms it had received over the years. We had the opportunity shortly thereafter to meet with Walter and Chuck and were deeply impressed by the depth of their commitment to the organization; Chuck's initial annual salary to serve as chief financial officer for OLPC was zero dollars, and Walter has guided the development of the Sugar software platform gratis for years. As good consultants, we could barely restrain ourselves in the face of the type of knotty, multi-dimensional business problem that OLPC represented, and our meeting with Walter and Chuck sealed the deal. Thus we embarked on what has turned into a fascinating and illuminating journey of capturing the complexity of the OLPC journey from idea to action to impact.

In the months that we've spent working with Walter and Chuck, we've had some of our ingoing impressions of the inconsistencies and challenges of OLPC confirmed. But we have learned equally as much about what OLPC—including both employees and the devoted group of volunteers who make up the extended OLPC network—has accomplished that have impressed and humbled us. Having journeyed with them again along the path they've traversed since 2005, it is now crystal clear to us—as both students and practitioners of social change—that dismissing OLPC out of hand was, on our part, a huge mistake. We believe that for others to do so would be a potentially significant loss for the educational sector in particular, and for social innovators of all stripes. We have much to learn from what OLPC has done, both their successes and their failures.

This book can be approached as a "choose your own adventure" for the reader. If you're looking for a chance to pick apart a theory for how to reform and revolutionize education, there is much fodder here for criticism and debate. Indeed, we conclude the project as converts to the tenets of their alternative, constructionist approach to learning (now that we fully grasp the theory), but also as ongoing skeptics about the practical feasibility of OLPC realizing its vision for change in the way it's framed and approached.

There is, however, another path the reader can take through the OLPC story: rather than approach it with an eye critical of the particulars of their program, one might approach it with a specific intent to learn not about *what* OLPC has done, but *how* it's gone about it. Its approach has garnered it world-wide attention, attracted the partnership of some of the best individuals and organizations from education, technology, NGO, and governmental sectors, and spawned many unintended benefits along the way:

- OLPC was one of the earliest pioneers in product-driven social innovation. In attempting to create a device that would survive in developing country conditions and be custom-designed for children, it invented solutions to numerous technical problems that eluded others for years and arguably sparked the growth of what has become the lucrative netbook market.
- Walter Bender initiated a large-scale free-software initiative, the result being the creation of Sugar software, interactive software custom-designed to meet the learning needs of young children.
- Chuck Kane has been on the cutting edge of exploring how to leverage market-based solutions and traditional financial mechanisms to generate capital sufficient to address educational problems at scale.
- Other members of the organization continue to push the envelope in a variety of ways, such as exploring ways to leverage bottom-of-the-pyramid initiative to drive educational change or how to more effectively enroll corporate partners in support of OLPC's reform agenda.
- OLPC's learning from initiating many deployments in markedly different contexts around the world has much to teach other organizations and sectors about how to build community networks and drive the community engagement and ownership required to create a foundation for sustainable change.

As a whole, the OLPC organization has engaged in a uniquely ambitious and far-reaching attempt to re-envision education in a way that recaptures learning, and ensures that those children who are currently underserved by—or wholly excluded from—the formal educational system will have a broader set of life opportunities. Disagree with its solution if you will, but it is certainly hard to argue with the vision of a better world that it holds out for all of us to consider.

—*Jody Cornish*
Partner at New Profit, Inc., a Massachusetts-based venture philanthropy fund focused on social innovation

—*Neal Donahue*
President at Lodestar International, an international development organization focused on facilitating multi-stakeholder solutions to complex social problems

ACKNOWLEDGMENTS

A S WITH THE CREATION OF THE XO LAPTOP AND SUGAR and the success of our various OLPC deployments around the world, this book would not have been possible without the work of a core group and the additional investment of a broad network of contributors. Given that the roots of the OLPC project date back many years and have links to a variety of sectors, the list of potential people to thank in this book is enormous.

DIRECT CONTRIBUTORS TO AND
SUPPORTERS OF THE BOOK

The authors want to thank Hitendra Patel and Ron Jonash of the Innovation, Excellence, and Leadership Center (www.ixl-center.com) for writing the case studies that prompted us to consider writing the history of OLPC. We would also like to thank the Hult International School of Business for its support of OLPC in its global case competition over the past three years; this involvement brought more clearly into focus the possibility of others learning from our experience as an organization. We would like to particularly thank Mark Rennella of Harvard Business School Press, who was the lead case writer for the IXL Center and who helped us in the early stages of framing the content and structure of this book, as well as connecting us with Palgrave to explore publication (successfully as it turns out).

In conducting the research for this book, we are grateful to have been able to call on many members of the OLPC extended network for insight and input, including Oscar Becerra, Miguel Brechner, and Carla Gómez

Monroy, who spoke with us at length about deployments, and Mark Foster, who shared his story of the early development of the XO. We would like to thank Elaine Negroponte for working with us to ensure that we fully understood the "origin story" of OLPC in Cambodia and sharing with us the extraordinary story of her ongoing work there.

In the writing of the book, we were also lucky to have wonderful support from a group of analysts at New Profit, the Massachusetts-based venture philanthropy firm with which Jody Cornish is associated. John Yang provided invaluable support both in researching the chapter on evaluation, as well as researching and writing the first draft of the Rwanda case study. He was assisted in his research on Rwanda by Julia Reynolds, the field learning and development coordinator for OLPC-Rwanda, who graciously offered time and insights to inform our case study. Kevin Greer conducted extensive research on the complicated story of Peru, including numerous interviews with Oscar Becerra to ensure we fully understood the human side of the story. Amina Fahmy helped us flesh out the unique story of Uruguay and more fully appreciate how it compared to some of the other deployments that we were reviewing. It is thanks to the work and great thinking of this team that we were able to identify some of the patterns in the complicated history of OLPC's deployments and tell a cohesive story in chapter 6.

THE OLPC TEAM AND EXTENDED NETWORK

When we first began distributing the XO computer, Walter Bender was looking for some way to acknowledge the many people who contributed to the program. As always, trying to make everything a learning exercise, he wrote the acknowledgments into a Python program as an example for children who wanted to learn how to use the language's dictionary built-in primitive. We again tip our hats to the 2005–2007 OLPC teams.

```
table = {

    'Hardware & Mechanicals': 'John Watlington, Mark
Foster, Mary Lou Jepsen, Yves Behar, Bret Recor,
```

Mitch Pergola, Martin Schnitzer, Kenneth Jewell, Kevin Young, Jacques Gagne, Nicholas Negroponte, Frank Lee, Victor Chau, Albert Hsu, HT Chen, Vance Ke, Ben Chuang, Johnson Huang, Sam Chang, Alex Chu, Roger Huang, and the rest of the Quanta team, the Marvell team, the AMD team, the ChiMei team, . . . ',

'**Firmware**': 'Ron Minnich, Richard Smith, Mitch Bradley, Tom Sylla, Lilian Walter, Bruce Wang, . . . ',

'**Kernel & Drivers**': 'Jaya Kumar, Jon Corbet, Reynaldo Verdejo, Pierre Ossman, Dave Woodhouse, Matthew Garrett, Chris Ball, Andy Tanenbaum, Linus Torvalds, Dave Jones, Andres Salomon, Marcelo Tosatti, . . . ',

'**Graphics systems**': 'Jordan Crouse, Daniel Stone, Zephaniah Hull, Bernardo Innocenti, Behdad Esfahbod, Jim Gettys, Adam Jackson.',

'**Programming**': 'Guido Van Rossum, Johan Dahlin, Brian Silverman, Alan Kay, Kim Rose, Bert Freudenberg, Yoshiki Ohshima, Takashi Yamamiya, Scott Wallace, Ted Kaehler, Stephane Ducasse, Hilaire Fernandes, . . . ',

'**Sugar**': 'Marco Pesenti Gritti, Dan Williams, Chris Blizzard, John Palmieri, Lisa Strausfeld, Christian Marc Schmidt, Takaaki Okada, Eben Eliason, Walter Bender, Tomeu Vizoso, Simon Schampijer, Reinier Heeres, Ben Saller, Martin Dengler, Benjamin Berg, Daniel Drake, Jameson Quinn, Miguel Alvarez, . . . ',

'**Activities**': 'Erik Blankinship, Bakhtiar Mikhak, Manusheel Gupta, J.M. Maurer (uwog) and the Abiword team, the Mozilla team, Jean Piche, Barry Vercoe, Richard Boulanger, Greg Thompson, Arjun Sarwal, Cody Lodrige, Shannon Sullivan, Idit Harel, and the MaMaMedia team, John Huang, Bruno Coudoin, Eduardo Silva, Hakon Wium Lie, Don Hopkins, Muriel de Souza Godoi, Benjamin M. Schwartz, . . . ',

'**Network**': 'Michael Bletsas, James Cameron, Javier Cardona, Ronak Chokshi, Polychronis Ypodimatopoulos, Simon McVittie, Dafydd Harries, Sjoerd Simons, Morgan Collett, Guillaume Desmottes, Robert McQueen, . . . ',

'**Security**': 'Ivan Krstić, Michael Stone, C. Scott Ananian, Noah Kantrowitz, Herbert Poetzl, Marcus Leech, . . . ',

'**Content**': 'SJ Klein, Mako Hill, Xavier Alvarez, Alfonso de la Guarda, Sayamindu Dasgupta, Mallory Chua, Lauren Klein, Zdenek Broz, Felicity Tepper, Andy Sisson, Christine Madsen, Matthew Steven Carlos, Justin Thorp, Ian Bicking, Christopher Fabian, Wayne Mackintosh, the OurStories team, Will Wright, Chuck Normann, . . . ',

'**Testing**': 'Kim Quirk, Alex Latham, Giannis Galanis, Ricardo Carrano, Zach Cerza, John Fuhrer, . . . ',

'**Country Support**': 'Carla Gomez Monroy, David Cavallo, Matt Keller, Khaled Hassounah, Antonio

Battro, Audrey Choi, Habib Kahn, Arnan (Roger) Sipitakiat, . . . ',

'Administrative Support': 'Nia Lewis, Felice Gardner, Lindsay Petrillose, Jill Clarke, Julia Reynolds, Tracy Price, David Robertson, Danny Clark, . . . ',

'Finance & Legal': 'Eben Moglen, Bruce Parker, William Kolb, John Sare, Sandra Lee, Richard Bernstein, Jaclyn Tsai, Jaime Cheng, Robert Fadel, Charles (Grasshopper) Kane, Kathy Paur, Andriani Ferti, . . . ',

'PR and Media': 'Larry Weber, Jackie Lustig, Jodi Petrie, George Snell, Kyle Austin, Hilary Meserole, Erick A. Betancourt, Michael Borosky, Sylvain Lefebvre, Martin Le Sauteur, . . . ',

'Directors & Advisors': 'Howard Anderson, Rebecca Allen, Ayo Kusamotu, Jose Maria Aznar, V. Michael Bove, Jr., Rodrigo Mesquita, Seymour Papert, Ted Selker, Ethan Beard (Google); John Roese (Nortel); Dandy Hsu (Quanta); Marcelo Claure (Brightstar); Gary Dillabough (eBay); Gustavo Arenas (AMD); Mike Evans (Red Hat); Ed Horowitz (SES Astra); Jeremy Philips (NewsCorp); Scott Soong (Chi Lin); Sehat Sutardja (Marvell); Joe Jacobson (MIT Media Lab); Steve Kaufman (Riverside); and Tom Meredith (MFI), . . . ',

'Pippy': 'Chris Ball, C. Scott Ananian, James Cameron, Anish Mangal, . . . '

}

WE WOULD LIKE TO TAKE THIS OPPORTUNITY TO ACKNOWLEDGE the community of people and projects that have made the XO laptop and Sugar software possible.

Most members of the original teams have continued make contributions to OLPC since 2007. For example, John Watlington has subsequently designed the XO 1.5, XO 1.75, XO 3.0, and XO 4.0. Richard Smith has achieved his goal of power consumption of less than two watts. Julia Reynolds has moved from an administrative role to becoming a key part of the local deployment efforts in Rwanda. Simon Schampijer is now the lead in maintaining the Sugar platform. Bernie Innocenti and Daniel Drake have been competing with Carla Gómez Monroy for the most time spent helping the most deployments on the ground. It looks as if Daniel, who is in Nicaragua as this book is being written, will be crowned the new champion.

New to the project since the original list was compiled are many people who deserve recognition and thanks: Adam Holt, Adam Hyde, Agustin Zubiaga Sanchez, Ajay Garg, Alan Aguiar, Alejandro J. Cura, Aleksey Lim, Alvar Maciel, Ana Cichero, Andrea Montoya, Andrea Palacio, Andres Aguirre, Anish Mangal, Art Hunkins, Aura Mora, Aymar Ccopacatty, Barbara Barry, Becky Young, Benjamin Berg, Bradley Kuhn, Carla Crosa Rivarola, Carla Sette, Caryl Bigenho, Carmen Rosario Ramirez Pantoja, Carolina Garcia, Caroline Meeks, Cecilia Alcala, Cherry Withers, Chris Leonard, Christofer Roibal, Christoph Derndorfer, Claudia Urrea, Cristián Rizzi, Cynthia Solomon, Dan Kilolima, Daniel Francis, Daniel Lee, Daniel Narvaez, David Farning, David Jessup, David Kaze, David Leeming, David Van Assche, Desire Rwagaju, Diego Uribe, Ed Cherlin, Ed McNierny, Edgar Quispe, Efraín Ferrer, Efren Ricardo Solórzano Portillo, Evangeline Stefanakis, Félix Garrido, Fiorella Hamm, Flavio Danesse, Frannia Araquistain, Fred Gross, Gabriela Mora, Gabriel Eirea, Gary Martin, George Hunt, Gerald Ardito, Gerardo Ramirez, Giulia D'Amico, Gonzalo Odiard, Graciela Rabajoli, Gustavo Ibarra, Guzmán Trinidad, Hal Murray, Harriet Vidyasagar, Hector Sanchez, Henry Vélez, Hernan Paches, Ian Daniher, Ignacio Rodríguez, Ileyn Bolaños, Ines Rivero, Iris Leonor Martinez, Irma Couretot, Irma Silva, James Cameron, Jay Lee, Jennifer Martino, Jennifer

Rodriguez, Jerry Vonau, John Tierney, Johnson Huang, Jon Nettleton, Jorge Saldivar, José Miguel García, Jovan Felipe Agudelo, Juan Saldaña, Juliano Bittencourt, Kalil Nicolas, Kalpa Welivitigoda, Karen Sandler, Katia Suarez Alarcon, Kevin Cole, Kevin Mauricio Benavides Castro, Kiko Mayorga, Laura Vargas, Leah Shadle, Lesly Ramos, Lida Vasquez Pajuelo, Luis Diego Fallas Naranjo, Luis Fernando Sanchez, Luiz Damiao, Magela Fuzatti, Maureen Orth, Manuel Kauffman, Manuel Quiñones, Marcos Orfila, María Elena Oviedo, Maria Josefina Terán de Zamora, Mariana Cortes, Mariana Herrera, Mark Battley, Marta Voelcker, Martin Abente, Martin Langhoff, Martin Oesterreich, Martin Perez, Mary Gomez, Mel Chua, Melissa Henriquez, Melissa Rodrigez, Mike Lee, Mikus Grinbergs, Mónica Báez, Norma Francisca Alarcon Torres, Norma Guadalupe Pesqueira Bustamante, Ofelia Solorzano, Olga Londono, Olinda Ruiz, Pablo Flores, Pacita Peña, Paul Fox, Pedro Cuellar, Peter Hewitt, Peter Robinson, Rafael Cota Rivas, Rafael Ortiz, Rangan Srikhanta, Raúl Gutiérrez Segalés, Raúl Hugo, Reuben Caron, Rita Freudenberg, Roberto Interiano, Roberto Rodriguez Alcala, Roberto Zamoras, Rosamel Ramírez, Roxana Beatriz Castillo Campos, Rubén Rodríguez, Saadia Husain Baloch, Salil Konkar, Sam Greenfeld, Sameer Verma, Samia Lounis, Sandra Barragán, Sandra Yanira Pérez de Umanzor, Sascha Silbe, Sdenka Zobeida Salas Pilco, Sean Daly, Sebastian Dziallas, Sebastian Silva, Sergio Romero, Sergio Hernandez, Sharon Lally, Silvia Kist, Soledad Tobares, Sridhar Dhanapalan, Stefan (Dogi) Unterhauser, Steve Thomas, Susana Acosta, Tabitha Roder, Thomas Gilliard, Tim Falconer, Tony Anderson, Tony Forster, Tony Sebro, Valter Cegal, Walter de Brouwer, Werner Westermann, Yioryos Asprobounitis, and the many others who have contributed to our mission.

Rodrigo Arboleda has done an extraordinary job of keeping the OLPC Association focused on its real mission: children and learning. Bob Hacker has been a great sounding board and someone from whom we have learned tremendously about entrepreneurship. Wanda Bender, who spends every day in the classroom, still finds the time in the evening to listen to and critique our ideas on learning. Of course, none of this would have been possible without the bold vision of Nicholas Negroponte.

FINAL NOTE

Finally, we should note that all opinions and conclusions in this book are ours alone; they do not reflect the stance of the OLPC Foundation, OLPC Association, or Sugar Labs in any formal way. As we noted in our introduction, we set out to tell the story of OLPC from our perspective—warts and all—in the hopes that others could learn from it and, with our experiences in mind, help to make a greater difference more quickly than they might otherwise.

ONE

INTRODUCTION

"You can have nothing in your pocket, and only the clothes and the shoes you wear, but if you have a well-educated mind, you will be able to seize the opportunities life offers you."[1]

—The Aga Kahn

IN POOR VILLAGES IN COUNTRIES THROUGHOUT THE WORLD, removed from the attention and conscience of much of the education community, a surprising scene is playing itself out: hundreds of poor children in drastically underfunded schools are spending part of the day working on small high-tech green and white laptops (the OLPC XO). After the introduction of the XO in Nigeria, a teacher literally threw the stick—used for corporal punishment in the classroom—out the window, as it was no longer needed to keep students engaged. In Paraguay, parents who had rarely been seen at school flocked to afternoon sessions about how to use the XO to support their children's education. In Pakistan, a ten-year-old used the laptop to start a photography business and was able to bring in supplemental income for his family. When Uruguay introduced the laptop nationwide, school attendance increased dramatically and stayed at these increased levels. And children are using the laptop in increasingly sophisticated ways: to search for information, write, blog, draw, chat, make videos, compose music, and even write their own software applications.

ENABLING A REVOLUTION IN EDUCATION

These scenes provide stirring and exceptional contrasts to the realities of education in the developing world in general and of primary education in particular. UNESCO estimates that 11 percent of primary-school–age children—72 million children worldwide—are not enrolled in or attending school. Rates are highest in sub-Saharan Africa and the Middle East, as well as in South and West Asia, areas with the lowest levels of economic development and social well-being.

Children who do attend often find themselves in crowded one-room schools without electricity, sharing a small number of out-of-date textbooks with their classmates. They are being taught by a poorly paid teacher who struggles to address the varied needs of the children of all ages who make up the school population. In many of these schools, the approach to education is verbal and highly structured; most learning happens through rote repetition of facts and information with the inevitable negative impact on students' skills, capabilities, and creativity. Children are literally having their natural love of learning drilled out of them. The proportion of children who are out of school, as well as dropout rates, are highest in these areas of extreme economic hardship where government per capita spending on education is the lowest.

From the perspective of social and economic development, a fundamental contradiction emerges. In our increasingly knowledge-driven world economy, it is no longer natural or physical resources alone that determine the well-being of a society; human assets are increasingly important. And it is the knowledge and skills of the talent in a country, rather than simply sheer numbers available for cheap labor, that makes the difference. As far back as Adam Smith, economists recognized that one of the key factors influencing the wealth of a nation was the "skill, dexterity and judgment with which its labor is generally applied."[2] Using a more broadly defined notion of human well-being, it is clear that those countries that invest in the "developmental health" of their populations—by ensuring, in particular, the availability of high-quality education and health care—are the countries that are most likely to flourish economically in the long term and in which the populace tends to have longer and more satisfying lives.[3]

And yet, formal education in the developing world is woefully inadequate. In fact, some might argue that traditional education—with a focus on the transfer of a set body of knowledge—is failing across the board. The main problem is that students are unable to make a direct connection between what they are learning in school and the skills they need to survive and flourish in their local economies. Education is not consistently seen as instrumental in helping students to reach personally meaningful future goals.[4] Consequently, many students, and in particular those whose time could otherwise be spent in the fields or otherwise earning much-needed income for their families, find themselves questioning the importance of formal education and ultimately opting out. In developing countries, this translates into a legacy of unchanneled entrepreneurial energy and untapped ambition, with individuals spending their time in low-value activities and perpetuating a cycle of subsistence living that betters neither their individual situation nor that of their families and communities.

OLPC'S MISSION

It is against this backdrop of profound social and economic need and educational shortfall that One Laptop per Child (OLPC) emerged in 2005. The mission of the organization is to "empower the children of developing countries to learn." The tool that we created to empower children was the XO, a rugged laptop specifically built to withstand harsh climates and the handling of young children. The laptop is preloaded with software specifically designed to promote exploratory learning for primary-school–age children. Our publicized goal was and is to achieve one-to-one computing, ensuring that *all* children in the developing world have access to computers as a learning tool.

We approached our educational mission with a hidden agenda. The focus of OLPC is ensuring that children in the developing world have access to something other than training that develops rote skills. Using the XO laptop, the goal is to support self-guided learning and exploration in ways that enable children to become critical thinkers, in-novators, and entrepreneurs. Going into the project, we acknowledged that we cannot solve all the problems inherited by the next generation. However, we can and must give them the tools to become a generation of problem solvers.

While focused on empowering children's learning through the me-dium of a laptop, OLPC was ultimately aiming to educate a generation of leaders and to create a foundation for social change. We took a bold position on the need for an alternative approach to education and were unapologetic about the potential role of technology, and in particular of the XO laptop, as an educational tool.

In 2005, Nicholas Negroponte, the MIT computer scientist who founded the Media Lab and OLPC, introduced the concept of the XO laptop in an address at the Davos World Economic Forum annual meeting. He described a four-point program for changing education in developing countries that included availability of affordable hardware (the XO), low-cost data communications enabled through low-cost satellite broadband and a local mesh network, integration with local curriculum, and involvement of local educators. In this same speech, he stated that within two years, OLPC would have distributed 7 mil-lion laptops at a price point of $100 each, a promise that seemed bold at a minimum, and to many unattainable, given that the average laptop price at the time was $1,000 or more.

In a time in which corporate social responsibility was a philosophy rather than a reality, we set out to find technology companies that had something to gain by working with us, and we successfully convened a coalition of for-profit technology companies across the supply chain to partner in the design and manufacture of the XO laptop at a price point within reach of developing-country buyers. In our six-plus years of formal operation, we have brokered agreements with more than forty countries and distributed almost 2.5 million laptops to primary-school children in Africa, Asia, Latin America, and other regions. The XO is instantly recognizable by people the world over, and the OLPC organization is among the best-known global not-for-profit organiza-tions. All of this was accomplished with a staff of fewer than twenty full-time workers. In the world of social change, where success is measured on the business side by revenue and on the beneficiary side by lives touched, OLPC has outpaced many other non-profits.

And yet, like any other organization that sets out to make a major change in the status quo, we are not without our critics. Forexample, at the July 2010 FailFaire, infoDev, a World Bank–funded program focused on the use of information and communications technology for development, used the OLPC's XO computer as a "trophy" given to the organization deemed to have had the least successful project leveraging technology for social and economic development[5]—a very public and somewhat backhanded criticism of our project. Because our goals started in such a lofty place, and because our launch was covered by media the world over, we have been closely scrutinized by education, technology, and development circles.

FOCUS OF THIS BOOK

How is it that in the opinion of many, OLPC has accomplished so much, but in the eyes of others, we should be credited with so little? Like any social organization that starts with the goal of changing the world, we have had some great successes as well as some failures. And we believe that many can learn from the choices we made. This book aims to recount our journey.

The OLPC story is one that will resonate with social innovators and social entrepreneurs in any field. Increasingly it is recognized that addressing seemingly intractable problems—such as climate change, population growth, and health, or the increasing gaps between rich and poor in all countries—requires new and innovative solutions that transcend the boundaries of established disciplines. In fact, as social entrepreneur Katherine Fulton explains, what is required is a fundamental movement to "reform or revolutionize patterns of production . . . with regard to socially important goods, like education and healthcare."[6] OLPC is a clear example of a non-profit organization with aspirations for systemic change on a global scale that is wrestling with tough questions that will be familiar to any social entrepreneur:

- How to balance bottom-up direct and tangible impact for individuals with top-down focus on the systemic factors creating the challenges with which these individuals struggle.
- How to strike a balance between a mission and goals that are bold enough to garner excitement and support, yet leave your organization space for experimentation and learning about how to achieve real impact.
- How to harness market forces to achieve scale around a social mission, e.g., through innovative funding models or creation of informal or formal partnerships to build markets or deliver impact.
- How to realize impact on the lives of those you're attempting to serve without creating dependence.
- How to build a distributed network to scale your impact beyond what you can directly deliver as an organization.
- How to define an approach that is clear enough to serve as an effective guide, yet flexible enough to allow adaptation to local needs and conditions. Relatedly, how to create mechanisms to evolve the core model to incorporate learning from local innovations.
- How to create a sustainable funding model without limiting your organization's potential for tangible and meaningful impact.

The book is broken down into three primary sections. Part 1 focuses on the origins and emergence of OLPC as an organization and a budding social movement: chapter 2 discusses the thinkers from education, technology, and social change that influenced the approach OLPC took to leveraging technology for education; chapter 3 presents a history of the design and manufacture of the $100 laptop, including the choice to be a non-profit, the original funding model, and the cross-sector partnerships that made OLPC possible; and chapter 4 discusses the creation of the Sugar software platform as a means of ensuring that the XO enabled exploratory learning for children. Together, these chapters will provide the reader with a foundational understanding of OLPC.

Part 2 provides the reader with a comprehensive and comparative look at a number of case studies from projects in Latin America, Africa, Asia, and the United States: chapter 5 discusses the top-down sales and distribution strategy pursued by OLPC and the challenges associated with attempting bottom-up social change in this manner; chapter 6 presents case studies that illustrate the variety of models that have emerged in deploying the laptops within educational systems in partner countries; chapter 7 discusses the evidence of the impact of OLPC projects to date.

Part 3 of the book focuses on future direction for OLPC and for social entrepreneurship as a field of endeavor: chapter 8 presents an up-to-date view of the evolution of the organization since its founding, some of the key challenges faced at present, and the ways in which OLPC is exploring and innovating to evolve from a social enterprise into a sustainable organization. Chapter 9 concludes with a call to action for readers, both in supporting OLPC and in engaging as agents of social change in addressing other social problems.

We recognize the challenges we faced as we set about changing the lives of children around the world, and we recognize that we made some mistakes throughout this journey. In this book, we set out to tell our story. In the process of writing this book, we have learned much about how to enhance both what we do and how we do it in support of our mission. We know we will always have critics, but we wholeheartedly believe in what we are doing. Readers of this book will have a front-row seat on the story of how we went from an idea to an actuality. For both ardent supporters and critics alike, this book presents both an invitation and a challenge: to set aside preconceived notions about OLPC and read the inside story of the origins and evolution of the organization.

PART 1

THE EMERGENCE OF ONE LAPTOP PER CHILD

TWO

THE ORIGINS OF ONE LAPTOP PER CHILD

"Where the computer's true power as an educational medium lies—is in the ability to facilitate and extend children's awesome natural ability and drive to construct, hypothesize, explore, experiment, evaluate, draw conclusions—in short to learn—all by themselves. It is this very drive . . . that is squelched by our current educational system."

—Seymour Papert, *Ghost in the Machine*

FOR MOST PEOPLE, THE STORY OF ONE LAPTOP PER CHILD (OLPC) begins in 1999 in the small rural village of Reaksmy, Cambodia, an eight-hour drive north from the capital of Phnom Penh. As described in a 2007 *60 Minutes* interview with Nicholas Negroponte, the founder of OLPC, the Negroponte family founded and funded a local school in this village. They gave the school laptops that Negroponte bought on eBay, provided a generator to power them, and set up satellite Internet connectivity.[1] The immediate results of this project were an increase in school attendance and family involvement in learning when children brought their laptops home to share.

Two years later, when Negroponte visited Reaksmy to see what longer-term impact the technology had enabled, he was struck by one clear result: the children were no longer limited in their learning to interactions with their immediate physical environment. Negroponte recalled that these children had become fans of Brazilian soccer teams of whom they'd previously been unaware. Through computers and the Internet, the children had been exposed to a broad range of information, culture, and experience. The interests of the children, and the context in which they operated, had gone global, and the very culture of learning had shifted. In a later interview in *People* magazine, Negroponte wondered aloud, "Has the tooth fairy arrived in this one village—or could you do this for every child on the planet?"[2]

For Negroponte, Reaksmy was an example of the transformative power of technology. From this experience OLPC derived what would become its core principles. It was clear that the technology distribution approach taken to date in developing countries—providing children with access to outdated technology through a trickle-down approach of periodic government purchases, donor contributions, or machines acquired through technology-recycling programs—would always undervalue the potential of technology to transform education. This approach would never give *enough* children access to the *right* technology and, as a result, would fail to change the culture of learning. The experience in Reaksmy suggested that computers—used correctly—could enable a huge leap forward in the learning of children in even the most remote environments. Also, and in contrast to popular opinion at the time, the project demonstrated that with some ingenuity, connectivity could be achieved in rural areas at a low enough cost to make universal coverage feasible. The experience in Reaksmy taught us that real impact would result only if the *right technology* was available at a price that would enable *all children to have access to computers*. (A detailed case study of Reaksmy is included in the appendices at the end of this book.)

Steven Johnson, author of *Where Great Ideas Come From*, notes that real breakthroughs rarely occur as independent and unconnected events—eureka moments. Rather, they tend to result from a slow maturation of ideas that evolve and become interconnected in new ways over time. In the case of OLPC, the eureka moment described in the origin story of the Cambodia epiphany—which created the momentum to build a rugged, low-cost laptop as a tool to empower learning for children in developing countries—belongs to Negroponte. However, Negroponte came to Reaksmy armed with decades of pioneering thinking drawn from collaborations with individuals at the Massachusetts Institute of Technology (MIT) and elsewhere about how to harness technology to revolutionize education and enable learning.

As Negroponte noted in a 2006 talk at TED—a conference series started in 1984 to bring together people from the worlds of technology, entertainment, and design to share ideas with the potential to change the world—"some people think the $100 laptop happened a year ago or two years ago, or we were struck by lightning. This actually has gone back a long time, and in fact back to the 60s."[3] This chapter provides an overview of the breakthrough ideas that drove the development of the $100 laptop and informed our conviction about how to transform education for children in developing countries. The ideas extend back to fundamental debates in education and social change and have their roots in the work of the scientists and engineers who first imagined the potential of computer technology not just for scientific and military applications but also for education.

A REVOLUTIONARY APPROACH TO LEARNING

In his 1993 book, *The Children's Machine: Rethinking School in the Age of the Computer,* educational theorist Seymour Papert opens with a humorous story about a group of time travelers made up of nineteenth-century surgeons and teachers visiting twentieth-century hospitals and schools. Time-traveling surgeons brought to an operating room would understand that a surgery was in process, but would be baffled by basic concepts of sterile spaces to prevent infection, anesthesia to prevent pain, and even the need to retain versus remove blood as a means of saving a life. On the other hand, a time-traveling grade-school teacher could easily step into the role of educator in front of a classroom full of students. Some of the technology—such as the use of overhead projectors and whiteboards that capture written notes electronically rather than with chalk and eraser on a blackboard—might be daunting, but the general approach to teaching would have changed little over the decades.

In the majority of classrooms around the world, it is a safe assumption that there will be a teacher at the front of the classroom, instructing the students by transmitting knowledge that they are expected to retain and play back to the teacher when requested. As children age, they will be asked to integrate the knowledge they possess with the new knowledge they receive. The teacher will operate within the Prussian system of education, one that embraces compulsory attendance, specific teacher training, a national curriculum, and standardized student testing. The format of this education—commonly referred to as instructionism—was the basis for education around the world for much of the nineteenth and twentieth centuries.

Despite its pervasiveness, many argue that instructionism is largely failing most students. In both the developed and developing world, drop-out rates are high, in particular among children from lower-income families and less-privileged circumstances. In an instructionist classroom, it can be difficult for children to make a link between what they are learning in school and anything that is of obvious and direct benefit to them or their families. For example, the choice between attending school and spending time helping to prepare food for sale to supplement a family's meager income represents a real economic trade-off. Without clarity about the practical benefits of making the sacrifice to continue in school, the choice to leave seems a foregone conclusion. Further, children who do continue with school are often ill-prepared to find a job and end up competing in the same market with others who elected to leave school early, often at some disadvantage. And these children are, needless to say, wholly unprepared to create new jobs and opportunities within their communities.[4]

In contrast to instructionism is the concept of constructionism, which focuses not on imparting knowledge to children, but rather on building a core set of skills that enable them to be problem solvers, critical thinkers, and innovators. Constructionism suggests that children learn more effectively through activities that allow them to discover and apply ideas as they learn rather than having ideas and information broadcast to them by an instructor.⁵ The roots of constructionism can be found in the constructivist theory of developmental psychologist Jean Piaget, who suggested that "children are not empty vessels to be filled with knowledge" as traditional learning approaches suggest, "but active builders of knowledge—little scientists who are constantly creating and testing their own theories of the world."⁶ Constructionism builds on Piaget's constructivist insight about the importance of experiential learning by suggesting that it is through active creation of tangible things that can be shared with others that learning truly happens. Children learn through doing, making, and sharing; therefore, if you want more learning, you need more doing, making, and sharing. Constructionism also recognizes and emphasizes that learning is not a solitary undertaking; children learn more and better in a *social context* in which they are actively involved in shaping their own learning experience and in which they do so through interaction with others.

One way to understand the difference between instructionist and constructionist approaches to learning is to imagine different approaches to a cooking class. For someone new to a kitchen, an example of instructionism would be taking a class from an expert that conveys the basics of food preparation and cleaning, knife skills, and the chemistry of cooking. Applying these skills while following a given recipe can create tasty results. Where the approach to learning edges into constructionist territory, however, is when we imagine creating a "playspace" in a kitchen where novice chefs are encouraged to try combining ingredients in new ways, discuss the results with their fellow classmates, and continue to experiment. The emphasis in constructionism is on giving learners the space they need to make their own judgments about what they want to do in the service of learning and creating.

Constructionism is often cast as the polar opposite of classic instructionism. However, rather than thinking in terms of constructionism versus instructionism, a more nuanced understanding focuses on applying the insights of constructionism to creating a specific type of learning experience for children. In this context, the role of the teacher evolves from instructor to guide or facilitator. By understanding that knowledge is not simply transmitted from teacher to student, but

actively constructed by the mind of the learner, the learning environment becomes less a one-way broadcasting of information and ideas,
and more an active construction zone in which the building blocks of
information and ideas are provided for children to explore.[7]

An easy way to understand how instructionism and constructionism can work together to provide a foundation for creativity is to consider LEGO™. Walk into any LEGO megastore these days, and you will
see kits of LEGOs that are prepacked with precisely the pieces you need
to build a detailed model that is outlined in visual instructions included
with the kit. Success in following the instructions results in a replica
of the picture on the outside of the LEGO box, an exercise limited in
creativity. For those who know LEGO well, however, the choice LEGO
made not to include glue in the box, unlike most model kits, was a deliberate one, intended to encourage children to take apart the models
they have built and put them together in new ways. By giving children
instructions to follow at the outset, LEGO builds their confidence and
gives them the basic construction skills they need to then venture out
on their own to create something wholly new. In other words, it provides just enough instruction to enable and accelerate construction of
a new model.

For OLPC, the insights of constructionism seemed particularly relevant for children in less-privileged circumstances. If one of the key
barriers to valuing education in environments like this is the disconnect between the information and knowledge being acquired and the
opportunities it creates for children and their families, focusing on
building problem-solving skills and innovative (even entrepreneurial)
capabilities begins to make sense. The experiential-learning approach
taken in a constructionist learning environment, done well, builds real
skills that students can then transfer to novel contexts. The emphasis
on making things that are tangible and shareable with others starts to
bridge the chasm between the classroom and the outside world. By encouraging experimentation and exploration, educators help children
begin to realize that they might experiment with changing their immediate surroundings as a form of problem solving.

At a more fundamental—and, to some, more radical—level, the skills being built through a constructionist-learning approach create an individual-level foundation for social change. In contrast to instructionism, which reinforces the individual as a passive recipient of a given social reality imparted by authorities of the system, in a constructionist learning environment, the fundamental lesson to be taught is active participation. Children are taught to explore, question, and experiment. They learn to be resourceful in bringing together different types of information to solve a problem, and they are encouraged to work with others to share ideas and craft new solutions. As Paulo Freire—the Brazilian educator and theorist—explained in his *Pedagogy of the Oppressed,* it is only by empowering individuals living in disadvantaged situations with the skills *they* need to change their environment that change is truly possible. Even in an exercise as simple as building a car from blocks, a child is learning not that he must adapt himself to the world around him (i.e., building an exact replica of a preset type of car), but that he has an active role in shaping this world (i.e., he has the power and freedom to envision and build the type of car he desires). This is a fundamentally revolutionary philosophy, and it is foundational to the approach that OLPC attempted to take, to change the culture of learning in developing countries as a step toward enabling broader change.

CREATING A "THING TO THINK WITH"

As a theory of education, constructionism is largely agnostic about the role of technology. OLPC, however, saw the potential of technology to be applied to education in a way that would support a constructionist educational approach and match both the learning needs of children and the specific circumstances in which children in developing countries live. Papert's vision, at its simplest, is that a computer could, for children, become a "thing to think with" that would aid in learning essential problem-solving skills. As with the educational and social change underpinnings of our approach, the core technology ideas trace their roots back to the earliest days of computing and to a fundamental shift in our understanding of the types of problems that computers can help human beings to solve.

From the development of the earliest room-sized prototypes in the 1940s, the hope for computers was that they would extend human ability for complex (mostly mathematical) problem solving. With the creation of the graphical user interface at Xerox PARC in the 1970s, the paradigm of files and folders, windows and icons predominated, and computers became primarily a tool to enable marginal productivity improvement in tasks for office workers. At OLPC, we have striven to reignite the power of the computer as a tool for interactive problem solving and creativity; this is at the heart of how we envisioned the XO as a learning tool for children.

In looking back at the specific history of constructionist uses of technology for education, a number of examples stand out that demonstrated possibilities on two fronts vital for OLPC. First was the exploration of the applicability of technology as a means of aiding constructionist learning for all children. Second was the possibility of leveraging technology as a means of leveling the educational playing field for children in less-developed countries who came from poor (and primarily rural) backgrounds.

As early as the 1960s, Seymour Papert began conducting experiments in using technology to help children think and learn. Working with colleagues from the pioneering technology research and services company Bolt, Baranek and Newman (BBN) and MIT,[8] Papert drew on artificial intelligence, mathematics, and developmental psychology to co-create Logo,[9] the first programming language written especially for children. Fred Martin, the co-creator of the now ubiquitous LEGO/Logo robotics competitions, described their goal as enabling people (including children) to "use computers to manipulate things more familiar than the then-prevalent numbers and equations."[10]

Papert and his collaborators aimed to create a program language with a "low floor" and a "high ceiling." In other words, a language that would make it easy for a novice programmer—such as a child—to get started writing programs, but that also had the power and the "sky is the limit" capability to be useful to an experienced programmer. And they were successful, in that Logo became very popular in elementary and middle schools and was also used in computer science classes at universities, as at UC Berkeley, where Brian Harvey has taught "Computer Science Logo Style" for more than two decades.

In its early days Logo was used to control a simple robot, known as the "turtle." The original Logo turtle, invented by Paul Wexelblat at BBN, was known as Irving. He had touch sensors and could move forward and backward, rotate, and ring his bell. Children would type commands such as FORWARD 50 to make Irving go forward 50 steps, or RIGHT 90 to make him turn right 90 degrees. Irving carried a pen, so children could make drawings on a piece of paper.[11] By using Irving, children engaged in basic problem solving, with Irving giving immediate, non-written feedback so that problems (bugs) could be spotted, all while having fun.[12] Later versions had a turtle-shaped on-screen cursor, which could be given instructions for movement and could produce vector graphics when given instructions to draw.

Logo was widely recognized as a breakthrough in teaching computing fundamentals to novice programmers, and its use has continued to the present day. Educators emphasized that by using a turtle, children are taught concepts of geometry by connecting what the turtle does to the way that they would move their own bodies. Through this process of "body syntonicity," children come to understand how an external object works by thinking about their own bodies.[13] In other words, the turtle became an "object to think with" and was a powerful way to introduce the idea of programming and of exerting independent control over your outcomes.[14] As Papert would later say, "Logo became a culture, a way of rethinking learning."

One early pilot project testing the potential of technology for constructionist learning within an organized school context took place in 1985 in Boston, Massachusetts. At the James W. Hennigan Elementary School in the ethnically diverse Jamaica Plain neighborhood, Papert implemented a project he called "Children as Software Designers." Each week for three months, children would spend three or four hours working on a project to build their own piece of software. The program built on notions that programming and debugging ensured that children would learn in a more complete and effective way that built their skills and sense of empowerment. Additionally, what Papert realized through the Hennigan project was that the computer both transformed the learning experience and quickly became absorbed as a part of the culture of learning. When asked what they were doing, children who at the beginning had answered "programming" or "working on the computer" very quickly began to talk about what they were creating, with answers like "building a skeleton" or "writing a story." The computer had essentially become an invisible but essential tool for learning.[15] Papert built on this pilot to launch "The School of the Future," a multiyear project integrating computers into the formal learning curriculum at the school.

Papert's early work resulted in the creation of computer tools specifically designed to aid the learning of children, as well as successful experiments that showed that technology could aid children in gaining sophisticated problem-solving skills. The question remained whether constructionist applications of technology were appropriate and applicable in less-sophisticated educational environments. In other words, could computers be a tool for accelerating education for less-privileged children starting from a lower baseline?

In 1999, Papert began an interesting exploration of the potential of constructionist learning through technology closer to home in an unusual setting: the Maine Youth Center, a prison for troubled teenagers in South Portland, Maine. The project focused specifically on exploring the potential for constructionist applications of technology to drive learning for at-risk youth with low motivation and poor academic performance levels. In partnership with David Cavallo of the Media Lab and Gary Stager from Pepperdine University, Papert worked with ten of the two hundred youth between the ages of twelve and twenty who were incarcerated at the facility for crimes ranging from vandalism and theft to murder. The participants had been ordered by the court to attend school and found themselves working with Stager and Cavallo in a one-room schoolhouse equipped with a PC, digital camera, scanner, and computerized LEGO blocks.

Learning happened without a set curriculum, with students collaborating on long-term projects that resulted in inventions as diverse as a LEGO phonograph and the creation of innovative computer games. As Stager later explained, the project was driven by eight "big ideas" including a focus on learning by doing; use of technology as a building material and as a tool for learning; learning for the sake of learning rather than to meet a pre-defined goal; taking the time needed to complete a job; and a level playing field between teachers and students. Perhaps the most important of the big ideas, however, was the concept of "hard fun."[16] For students with a poor self-image and a track record of misbehavior and low accomplishment, sticking with something that was difficult and being willing to admit and learn from mistakes were vital skills. In other words, students would learn much more than a set of technical skills: they would develop an understanding that they could contribute positively to the world around them.

Maine was also the site of early exploration of the potential for transforming the culture of learning within a community by ensuring comprehensive availability of computers for all children. As Antonio Battro, chief learning officer of OLPC pointed out, changing a culture of learning is not unlike immunizing a population against disease: you don't vaccinate every tenth child and hope for a positive result. In Maine in 2002, then-Governor Angus King, working with Papert, became convinced that "one-to-one" distribution of computers—that is, a computer for every child—was the only meaningful way to deploy computers to school children. His conviction resulted in the creation of the Maine Learning Technology Initiative, a state legislature–approved, $41 million effort to ensure distribution of Apple iBook computers to more than thirty thousand seventh- and eighth-grade students.[17]

The implication of projects such as those in Boston and Maine was to reinforce the potential of technology to transform education and to underscore that all children take to computers with equal ease, regardless of baseline skill level or the context in which they encounter them. The potential for computers as a learning tool was profound: it became increasingly clear that personal computers could enable children to "learn learning."

LEVELING THE EDUCATIONAL PLAYING FIELD

In addition to noting that innovation emerges when several existing ideas come together in new ways, Steven Johnson also notes that breakthroughs emerge most often in environments in which people are encouraged to explore, interact, critique, and collaborate.[18] In the case of OLPC, it was MIT, and specifically the MIT Media Lab, that provided the space in which the ideas of Papert and others such as David Cavallo (who cofounded MIT's Future of Learning group with Papert) and computer pioneer Alan Kay (who, among other accomplishments, conceived the Dynabook, which was the conceptual basis for laptop and tablet computers and e-books) came together to create a vision of how technology could accelerate education for children in the developing world in particular.

The mission of the Media Lab, founded in 1985 by Negroponte and Jerome Weisner (science adviser to President John F. Kennedy and president of MIT from 1971 to 1980), was to "invent and creatively exploit new media for human well-being without regard for present-day constraints." Members of the Media Lab team had spent decades demonstrating that computers could be powerful accelerators for learning for children, even (or perhaps especially) in contexts in which the formal educational system is lacking and the baseline skill and motivation levels of children are lagging. Building on this work, specific experiments were conducted within the Media Lab to explore the impact of constructionist technology in the most challenging of contexts: poor and rural environments in developing countries.

One of the earliest experiments in using computers as a tool for primary school education in the context of a developing country took place in 1982, in a pilot project in Paris that was funded by the French government. The well-known French journalist and politician Jean-Jacques Servan-Schreiber, building on ideas he emphasized in his book, *The Global Challenge,* founded the World Center for Personal Computation and Human Development to promote information technology in France. Servan-Schreiber tapped Papert and Negroponte to conduct a pilot project in Senegal, testing the ability of rural children to engage directly with computers for learning. Children in rural villages were provided with Apple II computers—some of the earliest personal computers—loaded with the Logo program. In the villages where Papert and Negroponte were working, there was no standard written form of the local language, Wolof—the script used was sometimes Arabic, sometimes Latin, and often a pidgin mix. Papert developed a written form of Wolof suitable for Logo and built a Wolof version of Logo for children to use. Despite these formidable challenges, the experiment was a success: children engaged in sophisticated problem solving. Similar positive results were seen in later pilots in Pakistan, Thailand, and Colombia, among others. (Rodrigo Arboleda, who would later become president of the OLPC Association, was instrumental in launching the Colombia pilot.)

In the 1990s in Costa Rica, the MIT Media Lab was involved in one of the earliest multi-stakeholder partnerships for education (MSPEs), which experimented in bringing together government, private sector, civil society, and academic institutions to enhance the quality and availability of education. The primary focus of the initiatives, which are coordinated by the Omar Dengo Foundation,[19] has been to improve education by leveraging technology in schools all over the country, including extremely rural areas and small towns and villages in hard-to-access areas. The initiative is estimated to have benefited over 1.5 million Costa Ricans to date in a country with a total population of 4.6 million. (It was in a rural township in Costa Rica that Claudia Urrea—who would become director of learning at OLPC—conducted research on one-to-one computing.)

In 2000, the Media Lab created the Digital Nations Consortium, which was specifically targeted at extending the benefits of the "digital revolution" to underserved populations across the world, including in particular children in developing nations. Digital Nations aimed to leverage technology to improve education, reduce poverty, enhance healthcare, and support community development.[20]

Taken together, projects such as those at the World Center, the Omar Dengo Foundation, and Digital Nations, illustrated that constructionism and technology have the potential to do more than revolutionize the learning of individual children. Until very recently in human development, chances were great that if you were born poor, you would die poor. Social and economic mobility were strictly limited by political, social, and economic oligarchies that condemn large swaths of the population to limited existences and unrealized potential. Underlying the emphasis on constructionism is the belief that, deployed correctly, education and technology have the potential to break down these oligarchies. Better-educated and empowered citizens have the capability to drive necessary social change, in particular in the context of developing countries. And children who have developed entrepreneurial skills are more apt to persevere and succeed in contexts where there is not a level playing field.

THE BIRTH OF AN IDEA

In the multiplicity of experiments in the United States and other countries focused on technology-driven constructionist education, some patterns emerged. These became crystallized in five core principles that OLPC codified about what was necessary to drive a new type of learning for children using technology:

- *Low Ages.* It is important to work with young children, between six (or younger) and twelve years of age—the years in which their core cognitive skills and their attitudes toward learning are developing. For children at these ages, the computer is both a toy to play with and a tool to learn with; the line in the child's mind between play and learning is blurred and the rewards of "hard fun" are reinforced.
- *Child ownership.* Children must own—both literally and figuratively—their individual learning and development. By having a computer of their own, children are much more likely to explore and learn in the informal, unfettered way that truly drives development of creativity, innovative thinking, and problem-solving skills. Children must have use of the

computers day and night, for their own use and to share with their families.

- *Saturation.* True success is every child's having access to their own computer—a form of "digital saturation" that can shift the culture of learning for an entire community. It is only when the whole community reinforces the importance of education and children receive support from a variety of societal institutions that social change is truly possible.[21]
- *Connection.* The ability of people to share ideas with and access ideas from others is a prerequisite for innovation. A successful program must ensure that children are able to collaborate and share as part of their individual learning process. Additionally, it must recognize the importance of community connectivity to the broader global society.
- *Free and Open Source.* The ideals of the free-software community—which emphasize total transparency, free sharing of ideas, and constructive critique to improve solutions over time—must be embraced both in the learning process for individual students and in the manner in which educational programs are put in place. By blurring the boundaries of learning, exploration, and creation, individuals become active creators of their own knowledge and futures.

An additional insight was that there was a consistent barrier to realizing the potential of technology to revolutionize education and drive development: lack of the availability of appropriate machines. The insight that Negroponte had in Reaksmy, and that his collaborators at MIT built upon, was that successfully shifting the culture of learning for children in developing countries required coordination of a top-down effort to design, build, and deploy appropriate machines with a bottom-up approach to ensure that the impact of these machines is maximized.

Negroponte took the stage at the World Economic Forum in Davos in January 2005 to present the idea for a "$100 Laptop" to be provided

THE ROLE OF THE TEACHER

An unintended consequence of emphasizing the role of the child in the classroom is that the role and importance of the teacher is either ignored or underemphasized. At the outset we focused on the child but failed to involve teachers in a meaningful way. In reaction to this this early misstep, we set out to increase teacher engagement: today, discussions with deployments inevitably revolve around teacher training.

to primary school children in developing countries. One year later, in March 2006, One Laptop per Child emerged as a formal organization with the opening of offices in Cambridge, Massachusetts. The focus of OLPC's work was "to create educational opportunities for the world's poorest children" to enable them to "become connected to each other, to the world and to a brighter future."[22] In other words, OLPC was based upon the recognition that education is a primary driver of social and economic development. The tool that we focused on to drive development was the provision to each child of a "rugged, low-cost, low-power, connected laptop with content and software designed for collaborate, self-empowered learning."[23] The organization would ensure that all children in developing countries had access to a "thing to think with" to drive their learning and ultimately empower them to participate in their societies and economies in a new and more active way.

LESSONS AND REFLECTIONS

It was not a given that OLPC would evolve as an organization in the manner in which it did: not only proving to the world the possibility of building a "children's machine," but eventually manufacturing what would become known as the XO laptop. The next chapters explore the developments and choices that drove us to build the $100 laptop, the emergence of OLPC as a social enterprise, and the development of the Sugar learning software. We close with a few lessons that we think are applicable to all social entrepreneurs about our vision and approach:

- *Be bold in your vision.* To many, the bold statements made by OLPC were considered an audacious stance, and the general consensus was that we were quite likely wrong. But these lofty goals when publicly stated led to more media coverage than most organizations would ever dream of and, as a result, brought money, partner organizations, and individuals to the table to support our cause. Would these partners have joined us if our mission had been less bold? Quite likely not. They came to help with a project with a clear vision and lofty goals (and great media exposure, which was a boon to many of them). So while there was a downside to making bold statements— industry insiders wanted to see us fail—the upside turned out to be instrumental in our success. We believe bold ambitions and innovative ideas are critical. In order to attract the working capital (cash, partnerships, and clients) necessary for your project to succeed at scale, you will need to differentiate yourself and paint a bold vision of impact.

- *The goal is not just to innovate, but also to create value.* Bold ideas might have some residual impact on the market, but value is not realized until the product (or program) is directly in contact with the beneficiary. Be prepared to run the distance required to see your project through yourself, or ensure that you have a well-coordinated relay team of partner organizations who can help you bridge the gap between an idea and its execution.

- *Gauge the distance between your vision and the status quo.* Look at the distance between the status quo and your vision for the future in order to gauge how far you will need to travel in gaining buy-in and support. Assess whether or not the general sense of what is possible meshes with your ideas of what is possible. Is your vision evolutionary, that is, an incremental improvement on current approaches, or revolutionary, in that it questions fundamental assumptions about possibilities and constraints? These factors will determine in large part the strategy you will need for garnering support for your ideas from funders and potential partners. Revolutionary ideas often impose a higher burden of proof; be prepared to go it alone in the early stages.

THREE

BUILDING THE $100 LAPTOP

"I can eat fifty eggs."

—Lucas Jackson, aka Cool Hand Luke

T THE WORLD BANK IN 2007, NICHOLAS NEGROPONTE and Walter Bender met with Joy Phumaphi, vice president of the Human Development Network, who oversaw the bank's education initiatives. In exploring the possibility of creating a computer that could change education in developing countries, Phumaphi was a clear skeptic. Born and raised in Botswana, her account of how she was educated as a child was a perfect illustration of the challenges inherit in creating a laptop to enhance education in developing nations: she went to school outdoors, under a tree; her school and her home had no electricity or Internet; and her daily trips between school and home involved long walks on roads that were either dusty or rainy. If OLPC were to build a machine that would truly benefit the children she held in her mind, that machine would need to work for years under the harsh conditions in which they lived and went to school.

Negroponte took away from his experiences in Reaksmy that enabling children to use technology to become better learners and problem solvers required provision of a low-cost computer that was custom designed to fit the learning needs of children, and was able to survive in the conditions in which these children lived. Such a laptop had not yet been invented.

The epiphany that triggered the launch of OLPC was not recognition of what this perfect laptop—which Seymour Papert had referred to as the "children's machine"—would look like; everyone within education and technology was asking for many of the same basic features. Rather, the real insight was Negroponte's belief that a laptop for children *could be built,* at a price that would enable the widespread distribution that OLPC saw as necessary to drive real change. At the 2005 Davos World Economic Forum, Negroponte publicly announced that OLPC would build a children's machine, and that they would have 7 million of these laptops ready for delivery to children in developing nations by the first quarter of 2007.[1]

In this same speech at Davos, Negroponte made another public promise that was equally, if not more, sensational: not only would OLPC build the children's machine, but it would do so at a price tag of only $100 per machine. Immediately the project became publicly known as the "$100 laptop." Negroponte's claim was viewed by many to be both audacious and unattainable.

OLPC didn't set out to physically build computers. We set out, first, to show that technology could revolutionize primary school education by cultivating in children new sets of critical skills and, fundamentally, enabling them to change their world. Second, we set out to engage the interest of the marketplace and incentivize technology companies to step in and scale the innovation globally. In the end, though, OLPC does manufacture computers, and in doing so, we took on and solved a number of critical challenges that paved the way for future product-based global social-impact efforts. The first challenge was designing a rugged, child-centric, learning-focused laptop and showing that it could be built at the affordable and promised price of $100. The second was recruiting a partner who would commit to building and distributing the machines at scale.

FROM PROMISE TO PRODUCT

Although 2005 was only seven years ago as this book is being written, to understand the extent of the challenge we faced at OLPC in realizing the vision of the children's machine, it is important to remind ourselves of the state of technology in 2005 and how far it has progressed since that time. In 2005, there was no such thing as an inexpensive netbook; laptop computers were heavy and fragile machines designed for business people and used mostly in offices. The average cost for a basic laptop was $1,400, compared to $650 for the average desktop computer. The machine that most closely matched the specifications of the children's machine was the Panasonic Toughbook, a rugged computer with a shock-mounted hard drive, magnesium case, and sealed-air design that was used in places like oil fields and combat zones; it cost more than twenty times the target price of the OLPC machine. In 2005, there was no concept of ubiquitous communications or mobile data. Mobile phones had not yet become the smartphones we use today—the Apple iPhone wasn't released until three years later; the first phone running Google's Android was not released until October 2008—and mobile Internet access was the stuff of dreams, with cellular bandwidth a tiny fraction of the speed most users enjoy today.

In stark contrast to the state of technology in 2005 were a set of ambitious specifications that experts in both education and technology agreed were required features for computers to be of utility to children in developing nations. Children needed a computer that could easily work indoors or out—in bright sunlight or in complete darkness—and that could survive in both rainy and dusty conditions. The machine would need to work for at least five years, at a time when the average lifespan of a laptop was less than two years. The machine needed to create its own network for sharing and collaboration where the Internet wasn't available. It needed to use very little power and have the possibility of being recharged by human or solar power if needed. It needed to be field repairable, so that children could repair their own machines (and, ideally, take them apart to see how they worked). And it needed to be safe so that exploding batteries or environmental waste wouldn't harm the children or their communities.

No computer sold in 2005 came close to meeting the requirements of the proposed children's machine (as of 2012, the XO is still the only computer that meets all these requirements). Likewise, the conditions to realize our vision of providing an affordable laptop with the capability for global connectivity to all children were not in place.

The consensus opinion of the industry at the time was that technology hadn't advanced to the point where we could solve for both the desired features and the promised $100 price tag in tandem. Achieving our mission would require both invention and innovation.

The Innovators

Although the technology did not yet exist in the market, Negroponte believed that many of the inventions required to realize the vision of the $100 laptop already existed within the Media Labs and merely needed to be shared with innovative companies that would find ways to utilize the inventions in their businesses and products. Our original strategy for tackling the dual challenges of designing the $100 laptop and finding a manufacturing and distribution partner was to "show the way" to existing computer manufacturers by creating a clear proof of concept and design specs. The initial assumption of the team was that when the industry saw this design and its impact, they would adopt the ideas and bring them to scale. This idea meshed perfectly with the industry consortium model that the Media Lab had employed in the past to share their research and innovations with the industry.

The seeds of what would eventually become the OLPC organization came together in early 2005, with the establishment of an OLPC industry consortium charged with creating the proof of concept $100 laptop. The intent of the consortium was to serve as a research and development "think tank" both to clarify the specifications of the laptop and to motivate industry partners to potentially step in to produce and distribute the machines in the future.

The original members of the OLPC consortium—Advanced Micro Devices (AMD), Google, and News Corporation—had signed on as founding members of a program at the MIT Media Lab to develop the machine, committing sizable financial and human resources to the project.

Every member of the OLPC consortium had its own logic and process for deciding to join the effort. The tendency of those organizations that we approached was either for them to join very quickly—typically

HOW THE MIT MEDIA LAB
EXPORTS INNOVATION

Perhaps the best example of a Media Lab industry consortium serving as a launching pad for successful enterprises emerged from work that Walter Bender initiated in 1992. Bender and his colleagues began to explore possibilities for new forms of digital newsgathering, dissemination, and consumption through the News in the Future (NiF) consortium. The work of NiF resulted in a number of inventions and successful spin-off enterprises, including eInk, the technology in the Amazon Kindle, and personalized online news, the predecessor to Google News.

because of the personal or emotional connection of a key leader to our mission—or to hold off, with the intention of waiting to see if we could build momentum toward their goals.

Intel showed early interest in the OLPC project but decided against participating; it took three months of intensive dialog before it made a definitive decision to say no. In contrast, Hector Ruiz, the chairman of AMD, took only four hours to commit the technology and engineering resources of his organization to the OLPC project. Ruiz was born in a small city in Mexico on the US-Mexican border and saw first-hand the power of education to transform individuals and communities. He crossed the Mexican border daily to attend high school in the United States and graduated as valedictorian of his class only three years after learning English. The mission of OLPC and the promise of the global impact of technology for education were personal to him.

In addition to AMD, the other founding members of the OLPC consortium were Google and News Corporation—Rupert Murdoch's global conglomerate. After recruiting this core group of sponsors, the team scoured the list of current and former Media Lab sponsors for companies that offered technologies or services that matched our vision for the laptop and the surrounding support systems that would enable impact. For example, Marvell joined as an early supporter, and based on its networking expertise contributed the WiFi chip and mesh technology (the hardware that allows the laptops to wirelessly connect to each other); when Red Hat joined, it was natural that it would contribute to the development of the laptop's operating system; and when SES Astra joined the team, it explored ways to incorporate its available global satellite connectivity into the OLPC ecology.

By the end of 2006, ten companies had joined the OLPC consortium, committing financial support and, in some cases, critical technical support. With OLPC at the center, and a core group of consortium partners in place, our team now had to deliver a working machine; we needed to move from an idea to a physical device as quickly as possible to maintain the public excitement and expectations that Negroponte had created—a powerful education laptop for an audaciously (and, to many, unachievably) low price.

The Innovations

The industry consortium enabled innovation essential to building the prototype $100 laptop in three parallel and coordinated areas: industrial design, hardware, and software. The industrial design focused on the design of the physical machine—all the things you see when you look at or use a computer; the physical design was critical in terms of building a laptop that was optimized for children and would depart significantly from the standard design of laptops to date. For hardware, the focus was on the internals of the computer, and in particular on designing a machine that delivered all the required operating features of the laptop while fitting into both a case small enough and light enough for children to handle and the strict materials budget permitted by the $100 promise. The software challenge focused both on getting the physical machine to turn on and operate efficiently and on maximizing the chances of children's using the laptops for learning.

Google possessed no specific hardware or software expertise related to the OLPC laptop and instead committed its resources to driving the industrial design track by facilitating the competition and selection of an industrial design partner. In March 2005, Google hosted a competition among industrial designers to identify a design firm that would head up the industrial design of the laptop. Participants were asked to present conceptual designs for a child-friendly machine that could operate as both a laptop and an e-book reader; it would have a handle to make it easy to carry; it would be rugged enough that it didn't require a case and would be strong enough to be dropped on the ground; and it would be human powered. From a range of great proposals—many of which met these standards, and a number of which missed the boat completely—one particular pitch from Design Continuum, an industrial design and consulting firm based in Newton, Massachusetts, stole the show. Its design concepts incorporated all the requirements, and its designers demonstrated a clear understanding of both the objectives of OLPC and the inherent trade-offs that would need to be made in building a finished product. One of its proposals, "The Wrap," presaged the tablet computer by five years: it made a sandwich of the display and the motherboard, which was then wrapped in a protective rubber sheet that included a keyboard and other peripheral devices. Another one of its proposals included an innovative hinge for the laptop that operated somewhat like a spiral-bound notebook and allowed the user to configure the laptop to operate in its various modes. Although the hinge was eventually replaced with the existing tilt/twist hinge from the Quanta inventory, Design Continuum played an essential role in bringing form and structure to the laptop.

At the same time that Google was pushing the industrial design, AMD, with its expertise in low-power processors, took a leadership role on the hardware-design track. One of its first contributions was advice that the project start by leveraging existing technology rather than reinventing. AMD's stable of processors offered many options to consider as the OLPC team sought to find a solution that would allow it to build a laptop fast enough to create the experience for children without blowing the budget. AMD provided the OLPC team with a prototyping kit for designing the hardware around the AMD Geode GX processor—an older and proven processor whose demand was declining in an industry that adheres religiously to Moore's Law.[2]

WHAT'S IN A NAME?

People frequently ask how the small green laptop became known as the XO. As part of an effort to design the original prototype, Yves Behar of the design firm Fuse Project included an XO graphic to represent a child as part of his sketch of the laptop. Negroponte loved the graphic and the association with "hugs and kisses." Behar and his firm were chosen as OLPC's design partner, and the XO became both the graphical symbol and the name for OLPC's laptop.

Jim Gettys, an experienced free-software engineer who joined OLPC as the VP of software, led the software-development track. The focus of his work was to extensively retool the standard Linux software kernel and GNU/Linux operating system to run faster and more efficiently so that it could be used on a cheaper and less powerful machine. Early versions of the machine using the Geode prototyping kit allowed the team to create the first working hardware and enabled Gettys and his software team to begin the process of bringing the hardware to life. Making the keystone decisions regarding the processor and retooling the operating system enabled Mary Lou Jepsen, OLPC's chief technology officer, to lead the team in developing a first working prototype. The objective of this prototype, which used a generic display and off-the-shelf components, was to create a physical object that would prove that the promise of the $100 laptop could be made real. Within ten months of launching, OLPC had a prototype to show the world. A bright green laptop was introduced to the world as a working prototype by the OLPC team at the World Summit on the Information Society (WSIS) in Tunis, Tunisia, in November 2005.

The prototype was nothing like the XO machine that we would eventually build: the insides were completely different, and the design of the case itself (including removal of the hand crank) would change as part of an extensive effort to add strength and robustness. Nonetheless, for many, with the showing of the prototype at Tunis, the $100 laptop was moving from a promise to a product—in the form of the little green machine.

WE BUILT IT . . . AND NO ONE CAME

The original vision called for OLPC to show the way to traditional for-profit enterprises. For the entire year prior to the introduction of the little green machine, we had been working on the question of how to recruit manufacturers to join the consortium or otherwise entice them to manufacture the $100 laptop as a for-profit endeavor.

This original approach conflicted with the motivations and market dynamics in the technology-manufacturing sector in several key ways. First, from our position in academia, we did not fully appreciate the extent of the gap between the state of the art (what was possible given the latest cutting-edge ideas and technology in the research lab) and the state of the industry (that is, the processes and technology currently in use). Second, we underestimated the private sector's willingness to take on risk relative to anticipated economic return, as well as the freedom any one firm possessed to drive innovation in a market in which so much of their success depended upon close interaction and coordination with other players.

On a tactical level, the reality was that our efforts to attract partners like Dell or Apple to join the OLPC consortium to support manufacturing weren't gaining traction. Brand-name computer makers didn't have robust sales and distribution systems in the parts of the world where OLPC intended to distribute computers. They didn't focus on the developing world for the same reason OLPC chose to do so: the majority of people in the developing world couldn't afford to buy computers, and those who could afford machines utilized private resellers in-country or imported from the nearest developed market. At the time, existing branded computer companies didn't work in the parts of the world where OLPC wanted to go, and they were unwilling to invest in developing the sales, distribution, and support systems required to both help OLPC and then eventually capitalize on any growing demand for commercial computers that might come from the effort.

No major branded computer company actually builds its own computers. The firms have great designers and engineers but when it comes to actually building the computers, every company outsources the actual manufacturing to ODMs (original design manufacturers) in either China or Taiwan. In spite of a sustained effort to find a branded computer partner, we acknowledged toward the end of 2005 that getting the laptop built and deployed would require a new, and bold, approach. While we had tried to leverage our typical industry-consortium model as a platform for innovation, we found no uptake from manufacturers. We were being pushed to move from designing and proving the concept to taking a more active role in realizing the OLPC vision at scale.

While our broader vision of leveraging technology to revolutionize education in the developing world remained the same, our role in achieving the vision was shifting. To make the $100 laptop a reality, we would need to consider becoming—at least in the short term—a computer manufacturer, responsible for the upstream design and manufacture of the laptop. Additionally, we would need to ensure that the downstream sales, marketing, distribution, and support were in place for the laptops when they were deployed in those countries with which we were partnering. In other words, OLPC would evolve from being an enabler of social change to being a direct actor in achieving the mission.

Making both of these shifts first required OLPC to become a stand-alone organization independent of MIT. While the Media Lab has a history of working with industry organizations to enable innovation, the university maintains a clear line of demarcation between research and commercialization. Since we were being forced to blur that line, MIT was understandably uncomfortable with the perceived conflict of interest between those working on OLPC and large corporate donors to the university. The administration did not want laptops to be "manufactured in the basement of the Media Lab" and encouraged us to make a speedy evolution into an independent organization. While the separation from MIT temporarily distracted us from our social-impact mission, the process was quick and smooth. From a financial perspective, the move was advantageous: even though OLPC now had to pay its own overhead costs, it was no longer burdened by MIT's requirement that 65 percent of every dollar that is contributed be diverted to cover institutional overhead.

When spinning OLPC out as an independent enterprise became an unavoidable reality, the first question on the table was whether it should be a for-profit or non-profit entity. While the organization embraced the power of the private-sector model of operating to drive rapid innovation, scale, and cost effectiveness, the power of a mission-driven organization to attract supporters and partners couldn't be undervalued.

Negroponte concluded that "being a non-profit is absolutely fundamental." In reflecting back on that time, he noted that "everyone advised me not to be a for-profit, but they were all wrong."[3] Negroponte chose the non-profit model for two reasons: first was the clarity of purpose—"I can see any head of state, any executive I want, anytime because I'm not selling laptops." For example, Kofi Annan's introduction of the laptop in Tunis was a direct result of OLPC's non-profit status, which allowed it to partner with the UN. Second was the ability to attract the most talented people and partners—as Negroponte explained in his 2006 TED talk, "You get the people who believe in the mission, and they are the best people." Non-profit status allowed OLPC to gain early traction in conversations within ministries of education and with heads of state in many of the developing countries of the world.

In early 2006, OLPC emerged as a stand-alone social-welfare organization [501(c)(4)] operated exclusively for educational purposes. The choice to be a 501(c)(4) effectively enabled OLPC to pursue the middle path of operating like a for-profit entity in some regards, but measuring profit in terms of social impact rather than money. With this status, it was theoretically possible for OLPC to partner with for-profit, non-profit, and governmental organizations to create an ecosystem that would ensure educational impact.

GOING IT ALONE

With the spin-out complete, we were now well positioned to find manufacturing partners and to scale from the single prototype $100 laptop into millions of units. In December 2005, Quanta Computers signed on as the original-design manufacturer (ODM) for the $100 laptop. Quanta is the largest of a handful of companies that physically design and manufacture computers that are then branded with names such as Dell, IBM, Apple, Hewlett-Packard, Gateway, and Sony. If you own a laptop computer, odds are that it was manufactured by Quanta.

If there is anyone in the world who knows how to build a laptop as inexpensively as possible, it is a Taiwanese ODM like Quanta. They had already twice turned down pitches to join the OLPC consortium; and yet within just a few weeks of the prototype being introduced in Tunis, CEO Barry Lam was convinced of the possibility of realizing the OLPC vision and approved a partnership with us. He named Dandy Hsu as the project manager as well as Quanta's representative on the OLPC board.

Quanta's partnership was a godsend for the project as we gained access to world-class ODM expertise in applying Quanta's own engineering and manufacturing expertise to convert a prototype and list of product attributes into a mass-produced laptop. Together we quickly created a mutually beneficial partnership. We got great advice and technical support for manufacturing, and Quanta got access to the substantial talent of our team. Quanta also negotiated a deal whereby the designs it helped create for the final $100 laptop would be owned by Quanta and incorporated into their reference library—meaning that Quanta could take all the technical innovations from the project and incorporate them into any computer they manufactured. This openness to sharing intellectual property and trade secrets came straight from our experience with the Media Lab industry consortia and was crucial in giving Quanta confidence that their company would recoup their substantial investments in helping to produce OLPC laptops. From our perspective, anything that helped lower the cost of laptops was in keeping with our mission.

Quanta immediately began to create value for our team. First, it reviewed the Tunis prototype machine and began to make recommendations for turning it into a viable product, always with an eye toward managing costs. Through the integration of its cost-conscious manufacturing practices and the introduction of existing solutions where available, Quanta gave us confidence that the laptop would eventually hit the $100 price point.

Like most innovative efforts at OLPC, bridging the gap between for-profit manufacturing and product-based social entrepreneurship proved to be harder in practice than anticipated. Our team at that time had little experience working with manufacturing partners. Not only were we asking Quanta to do bespoke design rather than the traditional assemblage of known components, we were also asking it to create a machine that worked with a not yet fully designed user interface, which made testing and optimization of hardware more difficult.

Almost immediately after entering into a partnership with OLPC, it became clear to Quanta that OLPC was not going to be like any other client it served. The impact of this was that the process of moving from prototype took almost two years instead of the more typical three months.

The slow pace of getting the $100 laptop manufactured was also complicated by the problem of constantly moving targets for hardware and software design. The typical hardware development model is that a computer is being designed to work on an established operating system like Microsoft's Windows XP™. In this standard case, the operating system and the API (application programming interface—the rules and language for how programs talk to one another) are firmly established, so the new machine is tested and made to work with that specific system. (Quanta was relatively inexperienced with GNU/Linux.) In the case of OLPC, both the hardware and the software were in flux—sometimes the software team would need to make adjustments to work with the hardware, and sometimes the hardware would need to be modified to accommodate a need identified by the software team. "This made the process long and complicated," Dandy Hsu said. "We'd make assumptions in the design, but later, when we got the software, we would need to make changes to the hardware."[4]

In retrospect, it is clear that the people at Quanta were not fully aware of what they had signed up for in partnering with OLPC. They might have signed on to more than they bargained for, but Quanta was also getting direct benefit from supporting the OLPC project: the

LAUNCHING THE NETBOOK MARKET

The OLPC XO laptop was the first computer in a new category, the "net-book." Netbooks sales began to take off in 2008 in response to a campaign by the telephone industry to market broadband service. Although the growth of the category was not correlated with the OLPC mission or market, its example gave encouragement and incentive to the industry as a whole.

innovations in the design of the OLPC laptop ended up in Quanta's reference library, and the experience undoubtedly accelerated the pace with which Quanta was able to offer their traditional clients small, low-power, low-price netbook computers.

With a manufacturing partner in place, the OLPC consortium had fully transitioned to an OLPC organization with the capability to produce the $100 laptop at scale. Just four months after the introduction of the prototype machine in Tunis, in February 2006, Negroponte took the stage at TED (a global conference on technology, entertainment, and design) to speak about our effort. At that event he was able to publicly announce that we were able to produce a machine that was capable of serving the needs of children in the developing countries at a price of $135 per computer. During his talk, he shared with the audience a non-functioning model of a design that was ready for manufacture, and that would strike what many had claimed was an impossible balance between desired features and low cost.

THE DEVIL IS IN THE DETAILS

While moving from the prototype design to the finished laptop involved countless trade-offs, there were three key design challenges that allowed the team to build a laptop that would be ideally suited for children, and that could be produced at scale at a cost close to the promised $100.

The team knew we'd need a non-traditional display that would enable children to use the machine indoors or in direct sunlight. Similarly, the objective of very low power consumption that would allow the machine to be used in areas without consistent electricity had always been at the forefront of the effort, but it needed to be made a reality in the final product. And finally, the reality that millions of identical machines would be released into the world meant security challenges for both the protection of the computers from viruses and malware and the security of the children who would be given these valuable machines, which, because of their relative scarcity and value, were a likely target of theft. The process of building the machine required the invention of wholly new technologies as well as the integration of existing processes and technologies; the result was a laptop that was a unique machine optimized toward children and learning.

Inventing a New Display

In 2005, Mary Lou Jepsen had been working on developing organic light-emitting diode (OLED) displays at Intel when she traveled to MIT to consider filling a gap in the faculty left by the death of her mentor in display research, Steve Benton. During this trip to MIT, Jepsen had a meeting with Negroponte that would prove to be a watershed moment for her and for OLPC: in a few short hours, Jepsen outlined her ideas for building a "dual-mode" display for the $100 laptop that combined the benefits of a classic LCD[5] with the power savings and sunlight readability of an electronic paper display. It became clear to Jepsen that the OLPC project offered an unparalleled opportunity to design and build her display within the context of a social mission that would have global impact. The combination was irresistible. Jepsen formally joined the OLPC team in January 2006 as the chief technology officer.

The display Jepsen had designed could operate as both a full-motion color display and a low-power e-book reader. This design would enable children to view the screen in a variety of light conditions and, if designed well, also enable a power-saving mode to extend the use time for children in homes lacking electricity. However, the challenge was finding someone willing to move from design specifications to manufacturing the actual display. Building one-off displays without a confident sense of the market opportunity was not the way the industry worked; OLPC needed a partner who could see beyond the standard model.

Jepsen found that visionary partner in Chi Mei. Chi Mei Corporation is a Taiwanese conglomerate of formidable size and diversity; it is both the largest manufacturer of pineapple cake and the second largest producer of LCDs (liquid crystal displays) in the world. LCDs are the displays used in most flat-screen televisions, computer monitors, mobile phones, and video game systems. Chi Mei Group's founder and chairman, Shi Wen-Lung, rose from poverty to build this major global company and become a leading philanthropist in Taiwan. The mission of OLPC resonated deeply with Shi, and within a month of initial conversations about partnering to build the dual-mode display, Jepsen and Negroponte returned to Taiwan to sign formal contracts. Chi Mei is yet another example of consortium partners signing on for a combination of both social motivation and the possibility of economic return.

Chi Mei assigned Scott Soong to represent the company on the OLPC board. Soong, who was really taken with the mission, worked tirelessly with Jepsen, often putting his reputation on the line, to bring her invention from design to manufacturing. The result is an LCD that is power saving, has great visibility in bright light and is easier on the eyes than most conventional displays. In 2008, after three years with OLPC, Jepsen left OLPC to start Pixel Qi, a for-profit technology company based in San Bruno, California, specifically focused on manufacturing low-power computer display technology.

Building a Powerful, Low-power Laptop

From the start, the OLPC team focused on creating a laptop that used very little power. Less power use would mean that the laptop could run longer and could potentially be charged off the grid, using human or solar power. It also would mean that the laptop could use a smaller battery, which reduces cost and size. Less power also reduces heat, which means no necessity for a fan or openings that allow in dust and moisture. (Most portable computers are called "notebooks" rather than "laptops" because they generate too much heat to be safely placed on one's lap.) But reducing power in a laptop is a tricky proposition; sometimes the power is consumed because a specific component needs a lot of power and sometimes the components in the computer are not working together efficiently.

The power problem we faced was, in reality, three separate problems: (1) the timing between the CPU and Jepsen's display did not work well; (2) we wasted a lot of power refreshing the screen when the laptop was operating as an e-book, where the screen might only need to update on page turns, every few minutes; and (3) computers spend a lot of time idling when they could enter a deep sleep. In January 2006, with the addition of Mark Foster—a self-taught engineer with over two decades of experience as a pioneer in the design of portable computers—we began to crack the code in designing a low-power laptop.

The most basic designs of the computer were already underway when Foster joined OLPC. It was immediately apparent that the prototype drew too much power to meet the objective of working in environments where the computer couldn't be plugged into an electrical outlet. Foster's goal was very clear: he needed to find a solution that would vastly increase the battery life of the computer. Just to make sure he understood how important this work was, Negroponte threatened to cancel the project if the hardware team couldn't find a solution to the power problem.

Through coordinated efforts led by Mary Lou Jepsen, Jim Gettys, and Mark Foster, OLPC was able to solve the power problem. In conjunction with a broader team and partners at Quanta, the three collaborated to develop a solution that focused on the timing controller—the device that traditionally managed the video on a laptop, but that was useless in controlling the display that Jepsen had designed. The team's invention—which they dubbed the "display controller" or "DCON"—elegantly solved the majority of interrelated display and power-consumption challenges.

The results of adding the DCON to the laptop were spectacular. The machine could now drive Jepsen's innovative display as both a full-motion, full-color display and a sunlight-readable e-book display. In e-book mode, power consumption now averaged below two watts per hour, which meant that battery life extended beyond six hours. The DCON represents true innovation that was critical to the success of OLPC and yet it was completely behind the scenes. The result was the creation of a novel design that makes it possible to reduce the power consumption not only of the $100 laptop, but of all computers.

Securing the Laptop

The security problems that OLPC faced with the $100 laptop were radically different from those faced by other computer manufacturers. In addition to protecting the machines from viruses and malware, OLPC also needed to ensure that the laptops could safely be given to and used by children while protecting them from two potential threats: the possibility that the machines could be physically stolen and sold and the possibility that, in playing with and exploring the machine, children could break the software running on the laptop or injure themselves.

Ivan Krstić joined OLPC in mid-2006, just as OLPC was putting together the first beta version of the $100 laptop alongside Quanta and Chi Mei. He was recruited to solve the problem of how to ensure that the computers that were distributed to children stayed in the hands of children, that they would not be injured in using the machines, and that the millions of children's machines around the world—all designed to connect and share with one another—couldn't be infected by viruses or malicious software.

Prior to OLPC, Krstić had been studying computer science and theoretical math at Harvard. At the age of twenty, he returned to his native Croatia, where he spent two years inventing and building an electronic patient-records system for a children's hospital, and another year reengineering that hospital's IT system. Krstić was drawn to OLPC for the technical challenges; by his own admission, when he joined OLPC, he didn't know that much about the organization or the mission. He was first hooked not by the idea that the XO would transform learning globally, but by three questions posed to him by Bender: (1) Can you make 100 million laptops secure? (2) Can you rewrite our file system? (3) Can you make it usable by six-year olds? There was simply no other place in the world that offered the opportunity to solve such difficult and critical problems.

To answer these questions and address all the security needs of the laptop, Ivan Krstić invented a wholly new type of security system customized for the laptop. This system, which he called Bitfrost, involves four software rules and one hardware rule. The first rule was that security couldn't depend on passwords—they're a non-intuitive barrier between the children and the machine, and that barrier is even higher when children don't know how to read and write. The second rule was that rather than acting as a gatekeeper to prevent unauthorized access to the machines by viruses and malware, the system would assume that all software was potentially dangerous, and any software was limited through a system of rights that prevented any application from doing anything other than the rights granted to it. For example, as a method of protecting the children, no application could activate the camera while accessing the Internet. This innovative move from gatekeeper to rules enforcer was the basis for Krstić's winning the TR35 award—an award given annually by the MIT Technology Review to recognize the world's top innovators—at the age of twenty-one.

A third software rule protected the software systems from being broken by a child. While children are free to modify any part of the software on the machine, an original is retained and can always be restored in the event of a problem. Giving the children a tool to recover themselves from mistakes without needing to get permission or help from a grown-up is a powerful incentive to take risks. The fourth software rule of Bitfrost is that the laptops need to get valid leases to operate at least once a month from either the Internet or a local USB stick. Stolen laptops that stop working have no value to thieves, and laptops that are reported stolen can't get a new lease to operate. Finally, in recognition that no security system is ever perfect and will eventually fail, one hardware specification was established under Bitfrost as a fail-safe: the LED lights that indicate that the camera or microphone is in use are hardwired into the laptop, making it physically impossible to access the camera or microphone without the light's notifying the user. To date, Bitfrost has been enormously successful: theft of OLPC computers is almost unheard of and there have been no malware or virus attacks on the machines.

THE CREATION OF THE XO

In November 2007, the first production XO laptops began rolling off the assembly lines of Quanta's production facility in Shanghai. This mass-production machine, marketed by OLPC as the XO laptop, was the culmination of more than two years of dedicated effort by a small core team and countless contributors and partners. In the end, the XO laptop looked quite a bit like other laptops physically; it was a bit smaller to more easily fit in a child's hands, and it was much more colorful than traditional laptops to celebrate learning and exploration, but it was still mostly a laptop consisting of a case, a keyboard, a battery, and a screen.

Underneath this only moderately different exterior, however, and behind the scenes of public statements and promotion, innovation and inventions occurred that not only allowed the XO laptop to become reality, but that also changed the computer industry in critical ways. Through the invention and integration of components in the XO— including the new display, power management, and use of low-power processors—OLPC shifted the industry's perceptions about the demand for low-cost computers.

Viewed through a social-impact lens, OLPC was an early pioneer in product-driven (as opposed to human services–led) social change. Through a close partnership of design, manufacturing, and original-component creation, OLPC created a technological tool that was purpose-built to achieve their original vision. During this time of invention and innovation, OLPC continued to consolidate the business foundation that would enable expansion from the original approach of "showing the way" to others to themselves becoming a computer manufacturer and distributor. In essence, we shifted from an assumption that we would catalyze creation of technology to enable social change to playing an active, ongoing role in the manufacture and distribution of this technology.

THE GREEN MACHINE

The XO laptop is not just green in its appearance; OLPC's focus on low cost, low power, long life, and field repair resulted in the most ecologically friendly laptop ever made. In 2007, OLPC received the first "gold" award ever given to a laptop by EPEAT, an organization that assesses the environmental impact of laptops.

In the eyes of some core members of the team, the evolution from catalyst to a product-driven social-impact organization was necessary to ensure continued progress toward the achievement of our mission. However, it did not come without sacrifice. This evolution required a significant shift in the mission of OLPC; as the number of activities that OLPC took on increased to include manufacture and eventually distribution, the scope of its mission narrowed. OLPC distilled its mission to embrace the recognition that the computer is the first barrier to impact, and that OLPC was uniquely positioned to solve this problem.

The nature of the partnerships that OLPC set up to ensure that the laptops would be built and distributed shifted incentives so that success became closely aligned with scale (i.e., the number of units produced and distributed). With scale as the key metric, OLPC began to be less focused on driving learning and shifting the culture of education in those countries in which they worked, and more focused on producing and distributing large numbers of laptops as a first step toward enabling learning. This focus on scale at the expense of ensuring meaningful impact was deeply disturbing to some of the original members of the team.

In addition to criticisms of narrowed focus and a "technology-centric" view of the world, criticisms emerged owing to OLPC's failure to meet the bar for cost that we had initially and so aggressively announced. In early 2006 the OLPC team held a country conference attended by delegates from all the governments that had committed to purchase the $100 laptop, to show them a functioning version of the computer. At this point, the machine was just powerful enough to run the operating system and the learning software; the amount of power required enabled it, in theory, to be human powered, and the estimated cost was close to $100—in other words, the first manufacturable design was pretty close to what had been promised. Coming out of that meeting OLPC was instructed by the government buyers to switch to a more powerful and more expensive processor, and to expand the amount of memory in the computer. Although in line with the desire to meet the learning needs of children, this decision effectively killed the possibility of OLPC's providing the world with a $100 laptop. By doubling the RAM and changing the processor, OLPC created a much more powerful computer—but moved closer to the price of $200 per machine.

This decision had ripple effects both internally and externally. While the delegates were happy, and OLPC was excited by the possibilities of this more powerful machine in the hands of children, Quanta was not pleased, as it effectively put the design process back almost to square one. As Dandy Hsu said, "Change the CPU and you're talking about a completely new machine."[6] Externally, the public expectations of a $100 price for the laptop had been so strongly set that to many this change signaled a failure of the project.

Nonetheless, as of August 2011, more than 2.5 million children in the world had access to cutting-edge, purpose-built laptops that they would not otherwise have. OLPC has evolved from being a university R&D consortium to creating a complex set of partnerships to enable the production, distribution, and support of XO laptops on a global scale. In so doing, the organization brokered new types of partnerships with for-profit entities that would enable the realization of social impact in parallel with driving profits at an acceptable level to make partnership attractive and sustainable. The technological innovations that OLPC drove in trying to realize the vision of the $100 laptop have paved the way for the entire laptop industry to reconsider approaches to power management and security. In the eyes of many, these innovations are in large part responsible for the creation of the netbook market.

The contrast between the enormous number of technological inventions and innovations sparked by OLPC and the reputation of the

project in the eyes of many is a fascinating case study. The public promises made by the organization in the early days were a double-edged
sword: on the one hand, they drew global attention to the project and
attracted best-in-class partners and talent to support the project in a
variety of ways. This was instrumental in OLPC's gaining traction and
accomplishing all that the organization has done. On the other hand,
it is easy for critics—coming from whatever standpoint—to point to
these public promises and clearly categorize OLPC as a failure. As with
so many things, the truth lies somewhere in between.

LESSONS AND REFLECTIONS

- *If you say you can eat fifty eggs, you'd better do it.* At the start
  of this chapter, we include a quote from the movie *Cool Hand
  Luke,* from a scene where Luke boldly claims that he can eat
  fifty eggs in one hour . . . and was consequently challenged to
  do so (successfully, it turns out). The power of a bold vision
  is, we believe, undeniable. Lofty goals are also important. And
  yet, if you fail to deliver on the promises you make, you will
  undermine your credibility over time. Those resources that were
  initially attracted to your mission will disappear just as quickly.
  In the case of OLPC, our bold claims, which had initially
  attracted positive global media attention and resources, over
  time began to undermine our reputation and make our work
  much more of an uphill climb. Do not promise anything you do
  not truly believe you can deliver.
- *Think big . . . and small.* Skip Barber, race-car driver and founder
  of Skip Barber Racing Schools, summed it up nicely when he
  said, "You go where you look so you better look where you want
  to go." Be sure you are consistently helicoptering up and down
  from the bigger picture and big problem you are trying to solve
  into the details of the solution you are creating to ensure they
  are tightly connected. In the case of OLPC, we became obsessed
  with the minutiae of the laptop and sometimes lost focus on the
  overarching problem we were trying to solve. We also failed to

pay sufficient attention to some elements of the business—such as sales and deployment support—that fell outside of our areas of core competency. It is human nature to focus on what we enjoy and what we are good at. There is a danger, however, that you will fail to put in place everything that's needed to drive impact.

- *Bet on the passion of people.* One of the "seven secrets"[7] that made the MIT Media Lab a vibrant hotbed of cross-sector innovation was our insistence on investing in the passions of people, not just their projects. We were able to bring together an amazing technical team to solve some difficult problems en route to realizing our vision of a laptop custom-designed for developing-country conditions. Despite some missteps on the managerial front, when we were successful, this stemmed from our recalling that "love is a better master than duty." With the right inspiration and general goals set, innovation and progress can come—powerfully and perhaps more swiftly—from the bottom up. Finding people who know how to think in the ways that you need, rather than those that come with a ready-made solution in hand, is often the key to breakthrough thinking and action.

- *Iterative design.* It is extremely unlikely that your enterprise will be wholly and rightly conceived from Day One. Be prepared to iterate on all aspects of your design: your product, your market, your funding, and your organizational structure. Innovation is not just building a prototype (product or organization), it is also engaging in a reflection about your work. Build learning into your enterprise by routine engagement in a critical dialog about all aspects of your work with both partners and practitioners. In these exchanges, your work is discussed within a broader context, ideas (and prototypes) are exchanged, improvements and alternatives suggested. Iteration helps you push your ideas further. You must learn from your mistakes (and successes).

- *Use a decentralized approach.* There is an expression, "the intelligence is in the leaves." Don't discount knowledge on the ground. The people you are serving with your enterprise have their own experiences and ideas and can be a source, not just a sink. Design your enterprise in such a way that you don't have to do everything yourself. Not only is spreading the load more efficient, it leads to a more sustainable model in the long run. And it lets you learn from the mistakes (and successes) of others.

- *Product-driven social innovation is different.* Recognize that product-driven social innovation presents different challenges from typical human-services enterprises and that there are fewer exemplars from which to learn. Things OLPC discovered the hard way include: you need to budget for false starts and mistakes; working capital costs (and overhead) will be higher and less flexible (so you may need to consider an earned-income stream sooner); product availability will be a gating factor for initial and ongoing impact; and testing and refinement may take longer because the product cannot be modified dynamically on a day-to-day basis.

- *Balance incentives.* Solutions at scale are rarely accomplished by a single entity operating in isolation. Increasingly in the social sector, you cannot do it alone. But partners do not necessarily have the same vision or goals as you do. They do not think like you and you do not think like them. These misalignments in vision and goals will result in bumps along the road. So try to view challenges from the perspective of your partners; reconcile your return on investment and impact with the private sector's focus on margins and risk mitigation.

FOUR

FUELING LEARNING
WITH SUGAR

"We're too concentrated on having our children learn the answers. I would teach them how to ask questions—because that's how you learn."

—David McCullough

FROM THE TIME OF OLPC'S FOUNDING WE WERE FOCUSED not only on designing and building a laptop. We also recognized that what children do with their laptops matters. For all the publicized focus and internal excitement about the potentially large numbers of laptops to be deployed, the engineering team was equally as focused on how the laptops would be used for learning. The questions we asked ourselves repeatedly were: Is the laptop capable of driving the learning of a given child? And does our program model drive the type of change that we want to realize in the culture of education in developing nations?

In his 2006 TED talk,[1] Negroponte made a public promise: he indicated that OLPC would not launch until we had commitments for sales in excess of 5 million units. Second only to the $100 price tag, the number of XO laptops that were actually delivered into the hands of children worldwide became a publicly referenced metric for gauging the organization's success over time. While the goal of one-to-one computing—i.e., a laptop in the hands of every child—had always been part of OLPC's vision, the pressure to "hit the numbers" pushed the organization to focus almost exclusively on the manufacture and distribution of laptops.

While Negroponte reinforced that OLPC is "an education project, not a laptop project," in nearly the same breath he emphasized that OLPC would not provide the educational software to enable learning, but would instead look to the countries in which the laptops were deployed to do this. The relative emphasis on achieving the goals of one-to-one computing (driven by the metric of scale) versus driving children's development (driven by the metric of learning) was a dichotomy that would come to define our future (and became the cause of a rift in our organization that would eventually take us in different directions).

The story of creating learning software for the laptop—which we named Sugar—is largely untold. The development of Sugar began in 2005 when Bender—then executive director of the Media Lab and a member of the original OLPC team—began a software initiative specifically aimed at increasing the probability of children learning with their XO laptops. The development of Sugar closely parallels the development of the XO hardware: the software and the hardware were developed concurrently, initially by the same team of designers and engineers, working under the enormous pressure of limited time and resources.

AN ELECTRONIC PLAY SPACE

When we hear the term "educational software," most of us think of a colorful interface of games and exercises designed to deliver a specific curriculum or body of knowledge that has been defined as important for children to master. Even interactive educational games, such as Number Crunchers, a number-puzzle challenge game created in the 1990s and often used to "teach" math facts in schools, are usually little more than animated worksheets trying to disguise the fact that children are merely answering questions by rote. The core idea driving Sugar is the notion that children and their teachers can do more than just use a computer for answering questions; they can use the computer as a "thing to think with" to spark *real* learning. Sugar turns the traditional educational software paradigm on its head, replacing interaction between children and rigidly defined electronic educational materials with a set of tools that encourage creativity and enable even very young children to program and modify those tools.

One of the key opportunities in developing Sugar was the chance to invent a new paradigm for human-computer interaction. Alan Kay once defined technology as "anything invented after you were born." This definition reminds us that children do not have any set expectations for how to interact with a computer—they readily adapt to what they are using and they have no innate affinity for the "Windows paradigm" to which most of us are accustomed. With Sugar, there was an opportunity to start fresh and revisit many assumptions, to break free of an existing paradigm and start over. Out with the old: overlapping windows, left and right-click distinctions, and double-clicking; and in with the new: applications running full-screen, hover menus, interoperability and data exchange between activities. The software designers were free to be creative on a whole new level.

On the surface, Sugar is just another desktop, albeit with a different look and feel. But there are things that Sugar enables that no other software you have ever worked with does. Sugar presents the user with a different type of "space" that feels more like a journal or a sketchbook than a filing cabinet. Sugar is designed to take away everything that sits between you and the information you are interacting with: there are no files, desktops, or passwords. In some sense, Sugar is much like a kindergarten classroom, in which a child can move fluidly between the block area, the trucks and cars area, the art area, and the playhouse area. Likewise, in Sugar, there is spillover from one activity to another.

Learning through Doing

Sugar focuses on helping children to make knowledge their own by putting it to work on problems that are meaningful to them. As a consequence, learning is something done *by* the student rather than *to* the student. In this type of learning, a child will not simply know the name of a thing and how it might be used in a narrowly defined context; they will understand its utility and its limitations. Put more succinctly, "You learn things through doing, so if you want more learning, you want more doing." This is not a new idea: much of the groundwork was laid by John Dewey more than a century ago in his work on experiential education and hands-on learning that emphasized active participation by the learner.[2]

In keeping with the notion of creating an electronic play space, Sugar is a collection of "activities," rather than a set of ready-made applications. These activities compel the learner to take action: to create something and to share the creation with a peer, a teacher, or a parent. To reinforce the idea that to learn is to do, each activity is named with a verb. Standard applications include those that will feel familiar to anyone who has used a computer: Write (a word processor), Browse (a web browser), Paint, Calculate, Record (a multi-media recorder), Read (an e-book reader), Chat (real-time messaging) and Speak (a voice synthesizer that allows you to type something in and then repeats it back to you).

THE XO AS A SONAR DEVICE

Not long after the first version of Sugar was released, Ben Schwartz, a Harvard student, stopped by our office to borrow two XO laptops. He wanted to test a Sugar activity he had written that measures the distance between two laptops. By combining the capabilities of the microphone and Wi-Fi radio built into the machine, he was able to use the laptop as a sonar device. His breakthrough application was aptly called "Distance." This creativity led to unexpected activities: for example, in Brazil the program was used in gym class to calculate the median height of the students and map their school.

Reflective Learning

Education experts agree that the best approach to learning involves do-ing and then stepping back to reflect on the doing: What did I learn? How can I use that? What questions do I have?[3] By helping children to ask good questions about the things they have done, as opposed to remembering the right answers, we are helping them to build the criti-cal thinking skills that enable them to be independent problem solvers. Without reflection, learning is an open loop, and an open-loop system can neither identify and correct errors nor adapt to change.

Sugar facilitates reflective learning by ensuring that everything children do with their computers is recorded in individual journals that include screen captures of their work. After every activity, children are encouraged to write their observations and reflections, which are also saved in their journals. From these records of activities, children can create portfolios—multimedia narratives that show what they have done, how they did it, and what their thoughts are on what they have created. Children essentially become curators of their own work. En-gaging children in telling about what they have learned as a "story" is a simple way to help reflection become a norm in their education.

By building upon the automatic accumulation of work in the Sugar journal, the portfolio process can readily be integrated into the class-room routine. It can be used as an assessment tool to help teachers, parents, and school administrators understand better the depth and breadth of what a child has learned.[4] At a "portfolio social," parents can be invited to view presentations and ask children about their learn-ing. The classroom teacher can add additional assessment slides to the portfolio addressing themes such as work habits and personal growth. This can become part of an archive that travels with a child across grade levels. Through the juxtaposition, the child and teacher can see what has changed over the course of the years, what trends are, and what areas need improvement.

In addition to the journal feature, Sugar applications are en-hanced by specific features that help children to collaborate, sharing information, insights, and discoveries, solving problems together, and co-creating. Write, for example, has a feature that allows peers to edit an essay or story a child might compose; Browse allows children to share bookmarks for pages they find interesting with other students; Record allows them to share photos in real time; Turtle Art lets them program Logo turtles within the same workspace. Interestingly, in many traditional school environments, this collaboration capability might be called cheating. For Sugar, in contrast, working together is a fundamental part of how children learn and is something to be embraced.

Understanding in More than One Way

Sugar activities encourage children to explore multiple ways of understanding a new concept or distinction. This is fundamental to real learning as opposed to memorization. As Marvin Minsky remarked, "Until you understand something more than one way, you don't really understand it."[5] In fact, the very recognition that there are multiple ways to solve problems gives learners a deeper understanding of the world around them and a stronger sense that it is possible for them to develop a new way to approach something. Sugar gives the child the ability to seamlessly connect ideas and efforts across domains. It is idiosyncratic and personal and specifically designed to promote the cross-pollination of ideas that is so critical to creativity.

Opening Up the Black Box

Forty years of working with children and computing has demonstrated that engaging children not only in using computers, but in programming them is a powerful means of driving learning. The process of writing and then repairing or "debugging" a program—which Cynthia Solomon (one of the inventors of Logo) described as "the great educational opportunity of the 21st Century"—provides a basis for active learning through trial and error.[6] In Sugar there are no black boxes: the learner sees what something does and how it does it. With just one keystroke, the Sugar "view source" feature allows the user to look at any program they are running and modify it. The premise is that taking

---

INVENT YOUR OWN ABACUS

As most of us know, an abacus is a tool constructed of a frame with sliding beads that is used for performing arithmetic. Sugar has created a number of different types of abaci to help children grasp complex mathematical concepts easily. It also lets children design their own abacus. Teachers in Caacupé, Paraguay, were searching for a way to help their students with the concept of fractions. After playing with the Sugar abacus activity, they conceived and created a new abacus that lets children add and subtract fractions. Sugar didn't just enable them to invent, it encouraged them to invent.

---

something apart and reassembling it in different ways is a key to understanding it.

Sugar also comes with a variety of programming environments that allow children to use a computer as a tool for creativity. These include many now well-known programs such as Turtle Art, which is based on Logo and allows children to make images while learning concepts of geometry and programming; Scratch, a programming language that enables the creation of interactive stories, games, music, and art; and Etoys, a multimedia authoring environment and visual programming system that is meant as an educational tool to teach children powerful ideas (primarily science and math) in new ways.

The ability *not only to learn with the machine and software but also to manipulate and change the software and hardware* itself opens the door to learning lessons far more important than those necessary to pass a test. It leads children to the discovery that they are what David Cavallo would term "authentic problem-solvers" in the real world.[7] Success at fixing a program also gives students confidence that they can apply the same skills—defining problems, developing hypotheses, creating tests, and executing solutions—to other problems they may encounter.

DEVELOPING SUGAR

Like the XO, much of the early development of Sugar took place in the MIT Media Lab. Development of Sugar began in the spring of 2006, in parallel with the work of the teams responsible for developing other aspects of the XO laptop's software, including device drivers, power management, and security. One might ask how OLPC—an organization of fewer than twenty people that had already taken on the daunting task of building the XO laptop—was able to create an entirely new learning platform out of whole cloth, and do so with almost no investment in software engineering. The short answer is that we didn't. OLPC solved the problem of how to develop the Sugar software with limited resources by attracting external resources—not creating them from scratch—while articulating a very clearly defined objective and set of measurable outcomes. OLPC built upon decades of research into how to engineer software to promote learning and amplified OLPC's staff resources by leveraging key partnerships within the free-software movement.

Our principal partners in Sugar development were a small engineering team from Red Hat, a major distributor of the open-source computer operating system GNU/Linux, and Pentagram, an international design partnership that does work in graphic design, identity, and product development. The Red Hat team, under the leadership of Chris Blizzard, an experienced systems engineer, was tasked with leading the software engineering effort behind the development of the Sugar desktop. Lisa Strausfeld, a former MIT Media Lab student who studied with Muriel Cooper, led a team from Pentagram tasked with developing the interaction design and graphical identity of Sugar. In six months, this core group was able to produce a basic framework for Sugar upon which a community of pedagogists and software engineers could build learning activities.

Both Blizzard and Strausfeld joined the team in large part because of their personal enthusiasm for the OLPC mission. Each wanted to bring their skill sets to the project, but also, each had personal ideas about pedagogy that they wanted to express in the project. Blizzard, who has a background in free and open-source software, wanted to bring some of the culture from that community into the classroom. Strausfeld, was interested in exploiting the potential of children learning through engaging in design practice. The opportunity to help shape the project from a pedagogical perspective was a strong motivator for every one of the early participants and remains an important motivator for participation even six years into development.

Rather than try to build everything themselves, OLPC worked with the free-software community to leverage many preexisting software projects. This community is made up of a large group of computer programmers who are committed to an ethic of user freedom to run, copy, distribute, study, change, and improve software. The community openly shares programs they have written with one another. Any member of the community has the right to use a program as-is, or to adapt it as desired, without needing permission of any sort. The key challenge for OLPC was working effectively within this community-software-development context without losing sight of the learning mission.

Sugar drew inspiration for its activities and the fluid interface between activities from observing how the free-software community collaborates. In this community, software developers chat, socialize, play games, share media, and collaborate on media creation and programming in both formal and informal settings. The Sugar parallels to the free-software movement are tools of expression, children creating content as well as consuming it, and a strong emphasis on collaboration, co-creation, and helping one another. As with free software, Sugar

---

NOW WE HAVE HACKERS!

When the current president of Uruguay, José "Pepe" Mujica, learned that a twelve-year-old from a small town east of Montevideo had programmed six entirely new Sugar activities for the XO, he smiled and said triumphantly: "Now we have hackers." In his eyes, this one child's ability to contribute to the global Sugar development community was a leading indicator of change and development in the country.

encourages every child to be a creative force within their community. Remarkably, approximately 10 percent of all Sugar activities have been written by preteenage children!

With the engagement of the core development team and a growing number of volunteers from the free-software community, it took only six months to move from idea to completion of the first version of Sugar. The team used an iterative-design process: rapid prototyping of ideas, followed by critiques, followed by coding. We went through two to three cycles per week until we reached consensus on a basic framework. It was at this point that we were able to set higher-level goals enabling participation by a broader community of developers.

Like the XO development process, which was going on in parallel, the software-development process required ongoing efforts to solve knotty and often unprecedented technical problems. To wrestle with these, the OLPC, Red Hat, and Pentagram teams met face-to-face on a biweekly basis. The broader development community, which was dispersed across five continents, was engaged in addressing the same problems and met 24/7 in multilingual online chat forums. This was a global movement: the lead developer lived outside of Milan, Italy, the lead community contributor lived in Siberia, and the principal testing team operated out of a coffee shop in Wellington, New Zealand. Significant contributions were made by a high school student from Wunstorf, Germany, an energy-management consultant living in Melbourne, Australia, and a student at the University of San Carlos in Brazil. The use of modern software-development tools, such as distributed source-code management and wikis enabled members of the development community to collaborate anywhere and at any time. We were also able to pilot Sugar in a wide range of contexts, getting hands-on experience and feedback in schools in Nigeria, Thailand, Cambodia, and Brazil.

Sugar was designed so that new uses emerging from the community could easily be incorporated. The journal was the brainchild of Ivan Krstić, who also designed OLPC's security model. Popular activities came from community volunteers such as Brian Silverman, a long-time collaborator of Papert's who created Turtle Art, and Alan Kay and the Viewpoint team who created the Etoys learning environment.

Others were commissioned from specific individuals, including a multimedia activity called Record written by Erik Blankinship and Bakhtiar Mikhak; the Sugar word processor, Write, which was based on Abiword and written by J. M. Maurer; the TamTam musical activity suite written by Jean Piché and his students at the University of Montreal; and some constructionist games from Harel's MamaMedia group that were "Sugarized" by Morgan Collett and Carlos Neves.

Sugar was explicitly designed by OLPC to be augmented and amplified by its community and the end users: once these initial examples were published, the floodgates opened and activities began to come in unsolicited. While we had the advantage of a highly publicized project—OLPC was the subject of almost daily international news coverage—we did not necessarily have direct access to the highly skilled software-development community we needed in order to grow. We therefore did outreach in the forums where software developers hung out. In free software, that is primarily in chat rooms and at conferences. Blizzard and the Red Hat team established an Internet relay chat (IRC) channel for the project that soon attracted nearly one hundred concurrent users. Jim Gettys spend a great deal of his time attending free-software conferences, focusing especially on conferences in regions where OLPC was targeting deployments, in order to solicit volunteers. We also used word of mouth, leveraging both the MIT alumni network and friends and colleagues from industry.

Sugar was also designed so that end users could make contributions to the software itself. One of the stories that exemplifies this took place in Abuja, a city in Nigeria that became that nation's capital in 1991 (as a neutral location it was hoped that it might placate some of the ethnic and religious divisions that have beset the county). Abuja was the site of the first OLPC pilot for the beta XO laptop and Sugar. While teachers and students took to the laptop quickly in general, they did confront some problems. The most notable of these was that the Write word-processor activity did not have a spelling dictionary in Igbo, the dialect used in this particular classroom (and one of the more than three hundred languages currently spoken in Nigeria). From a conventional software-development standpoint, solving this problem would be prohibitively expensive, demanding huge resources. But for children in Abuja equipped with Sugar, the answer was relatively simple. Confronted with the problem of lacking a dictionary in Igbo, they made their own Igbo dictionary. The free-software ethic built into Sugar enabled local control and innovation.

By the end of 2006—less than six months after the idea was born—Sugar had a basic system running that included all of the basic activities: Write, Browse, Read, Paint, etc. By the end of 2009, Sugar had hundreds of activities contributed by thousands of developers around the world, and the ongoing engagement of a global group of developers, teachers, and students.

A FORK IN THE ROAD

Despite the fast progress and impressive accomplishments of the team that created Sugar, within OLPC there were real and growing concerns about creating a new user interface for the laptop and resistance to expending resources on its development. At the same time, XO laptop sales were failing to meet expectations. While the development process for the XO resulted in the first machine being finished and ready to ship in November 2007, the original partnerships that we had counted on for the target 5 million laptop sales had not materialized. Instead, by the beginning of 2008, OLPC had commitments from Uruguay, Alabama, Peru, and Mexico that totaled only 425,000 machines. Being so far below projections was putting some pressure on the organization. We had been funding development with membership fees from the OLPC industry consortium; even with those funds taken into account, we had been sustaining a burn rate that exceeded our income. Our forward spending was with the expectation that these costs would eventually be balanced out by funds received from deployment contracts.

While we did not panic when confronted with a slow sales cycle, we did begin to look for explanations. Some of the fallout was the result of events beyond our control: a coup in Thailand, a personal tragedy in Pakistan. Some was due to lackluster commitment on behalf of our partners: President Olusegun Obasanjo of Nigeria, presumably looking for excuses for inaction, said he would buy the computers for Nigeria only when they cost $100. Further, competitors from the commercial sector were working hard to undermine our efforts, most effectively in Brazil and Argentina. Nonetheless, we were concerned that while our mission was well received for the most part, our product was not meeting the needs or expectations of the market.

The OLPC board was not convinced that investing in a custom and unique software-user interface was a realistic way of supporting OLPC's goal of shipping large numbers of laptops. They had serious doubts about the ability of OLPC to penetrate the education market without offering a more conventional approach to software and pedagogy. For governments that considered adopting the notion of one-to-one computing a big step, adding the uncertainty of unfamiliar software made the decision all the more difficult. Fueling the tension was a report from a meeting that OLPC had with the Egyptian minister of education, in which he was asked if Microsoft Windows could be run on the XO laptop (the answer at that point was no). Facing such requests, Negroponte announced at the February 2008 OLPC board meeting that the organization would refocus its efforts around Windows. Much of the board breathed a sigh of relief, as they predicted that switching to Windows would mean significant growth in the number of laptops deployed.

Meanwhile, market demand for cheaper, lighter laptops—netbooks—was growing and that industry was gaining momentum. While OLPC was the market leader, it was clear that there would be many competitors emerging in the near future, all of which had potential as platforms for educating children. The Sugar community and many at OLPC considered the question: "If we believe that Sugar offers a great learning experience, why not make it available to children regardless of which computer they are using?" This was a clear instance of divergent theories of change.

After the February 2008 board meeting, OLPC and the Sugar community split. One month later, Sugar Labs was founded as an independent non-profit organization that would continue to drive the development and dissemination of the Sugar learning software. In the immediate aftermath of the split, OLPC rapidly expanded its staff, going from fewer than twenty full-time employees to nearly sixty. However, only a few of these were actively working on user-interfacing software. Sugar development did not lose any of its momentum, as the volunteer community continued its efforts and the handful of OLPC engineers who had been working on Sugar—some of whom were founding members of Sugar Labs—pressed on as well. Meanwhile, Negroponte was convinced that a switch to Windows would result in hundreds of millions of laptop sales. Bender was convinced that Sugar would have value even without the OLPC-installed base. At the management level, there was a tacit agreement to go our separate ways.

Tension at OLPC did not diminish after the split with Sugar Labs; there was a continued internal debate between lofty aspirations and tactics. One year later, there was a further split that resulted in the creation of the OLPC Foundation and the OLPC Association as separate entities. The Foundation, run by Negroponte, was tasked with the "big picture" and future thinking. The Association, run by Rodrigo Arboleda, was tasked with the practical work of driving impact, defined as getting the laptop built, getting tools onto the laptop to enable learning, and getting the laptop into the hands of children and their teachers.

It is not unusual that the founders of an idea or movement have different ideas and that their paths diverge. This is just as likely to occur in a social enterprise as in a commercial enterprise. While breaking up is hard to do, its consequences can be positive. The anticipated boost in sales from Windows never materialized, and OLPC still represents 95 percent of the Sugar user base. Three years after the split, despite having had differences of opinion about tactics, OLPC Foundation, OLPC Association, and Sugar Labs all work together closely, each playing a unique role in advancing the opportunities for learning from independent but synergistic perspectives. OLPC Foundation drives future hardware development; OLPC Association builds and distributes laptops; Sugar Labs provides the software that is run on those laptops; and the OLPC and Sugar communities work together with local deployments to support children and their teachers.

SUGAR LABS, PLURAL

In the aftermath of the split with OLPC, creating a new organization to develop and maintain the Sugar software was straightforward. The founding members consisted of a small core of developers who were dedicated to the project, including some members of the original OLPC engineering team. The Sugar community suffered very little attrition after the split with OLPC; rather, when Sugar Labs was created, some new developers joined who were inspired by the new direction. Sugar Labs is a member project of the Software Freedom Conservancy (SFC), a non-profit organization that helps "promote, improve, develop, and defend" free-software projects. The SFC provides a non-profit home for Sugar Labs and it takes care of any project needs not directly related to software development. The decision to move the project to the SFC was in large part motivated by the potential for networking provided by the alliance with other free-software projects. Only by building partnerships has Sugar Labs been able to operate with a balance sheet of zero revenue and zero cost.

The real challenge that we faced was how to create an organization that would support our learning mission, enable ongoing innovation, and allow for local contextualization and appropriation. The key innovation that Sugar Labs embraced was creating a flexible model that supports and encourages the creation of local and regional labs. The local labs take whatever form makes sense in each country's or community's context, including, in some cases, being established as for-profit enterprises, which Sugar Labs "central" cannot do. These labs were originally encouraged in those countries in which the XO laptop was being deployed, to ensure that Sugar meshed with the local culture and to give local communities a channel for contributing to Sugar's ongoing evolution. Sugar Labs affiliates exist in most of the countries in which OLPC has major deployments—Uruguay, Argentina, Paraguay, Peru—and in some of the countries in which smaller numbers of laptops have been deployed—such as Colombia and Chile. Local lab members are on a par with their global colleagues: everyone learns to cooperate, compete, and contribute in a global marketplace. There are also Sugar Labs that exist without direct affiliation to a country-level deployment, such as the Washington, DC, lab, which rallies its members to support Sugar from technical, pedagogical, and marketing perspectives.

These regional labs play a number of important roles in supporting Sugar's success. The first is providing for communication between local communities and the global developer community. The constant flow of information back and forth between the global and local Sugar labs is mutually beneficial, reinforcing the mission and core principles and circulating new ideas and new energy as new challenges are encountered. Regional and local labs also develop new activities for Sugar; overall, local labs are the source of an increasingly large percentage of all Sugar activities.

When working with local groups, two questions often arise: how to recruit and how to ensure quality. In the case of Sugar, the recruitment occurs through multiple channels: there is interest driven by the OLPC deployments; local free-software developers are often looking for a local outlet for their talents; and local universities are looking for ways to both engage their students in social action and provide tangible outlets for their engineering students. Quality control operates in the manner of all free-software projects: software is submitted "upstream"[8] to the maintainers, who vet it for quality. High-quality work gets absorbed into the project at a global level. But whether or not software developed locally is suitable for deployment is ultimately a decision made by the deployments themselves. The structure of Sugar is such that local repositories of activities (e.g., the local "App Store") are on an equal footing with the global repository.

Sugar development began in 2006 under the OLPC umbrella. It was spun out as an independent non-profit, Sugar Labs, in 2008. The lessons of Sugar's development for non-profits and social entrepreneurs are rich. We have a balance sheet of zero revenue and zero cost and a 100 percent volunteer staff numbering in the thousands. We have consistently been producing a new release of the software every six months. Our software is available in more than twenty-five languages and is used by almost 3 million children in more than forty countries

---

FUELING ENTREPRENEURISM WITH SUGAR

In Uruguay, Plan Ceibal was developed to deploy one laptop per child throughout the entire country. A by-product of this initiative has been the creation of new jobs: everything from logistics and technology support to the installation of power and network infrastructure to teacher training and curriculum development. For just this one educational initiative, more than three hundred new jobs were created. And not just for local consumption: Plan Ceibal personnel consult internationally; for example, they helped design and implement a deployment in the Nagorno-Karabakh Republic.

---

each day. These statistics are impressive for any software development organization, let alone a volunteer-led non-profit foundation.

LESSONS AND REFLECTIONS

The experiences of Sugar Labs, including its parting of the way with OLPC, provide some object lessons for social entrepreneurs.

- *Necessary tension between organizational sustainability and widespread impact.* Social enterprises start out by focusing on a social problem and desired impact and create an organization to serve as the tool for driving impact. Over time, it is not uncommon to focus on the sustainability of the organization just as much as the end-state impact about which you care. In the case of OLPC, the original public promise to achieve the $100 price point and deliver millions of laptops—which had been so effective in garnering attention and resources—grew to overshadow the impact on learning that was the original focus. In the case of Sugar, the choice to make the software freely available to anyone with a computer had the potential to dilute a key strategic advantage of OLPC in the marketplace. On the other hand, it also created the opportunity to drive impact in a broader set of countries where the XOs were not deployed. By embracing Sugar Labs, the more narrowly defined interests of the OLPC Association, which aimed to maximize the number of computers sold, evolved into a solution that could again focus on learning. This tension of balancing the requirement to create a sustainable funding base with maintaining focus on addressing a system-level social need should be familiar to any social entrepreneur.

- *Balancing control and autonomy.* Deploying Sugar through the global-local Sugar Labs networks provides a promising model for how social entrepreneurs can successfully scale their efforts. By creating a structured platform and approach to development, Sugar effectively created "guardrails" that allowed for local customization and innovation that would contribute to the overall mission. The deliberate effort to hand over control (and responsibility) for Sugar to local and regional groups led to self-determination and local relevancy. It also met a core need of the central organization: without local input and control, Sugar Labs could not ensure that Sugar remained relevant and up-to-date for the needs of specific populations and, ultimately, that it had an impact. The interdependence of local and global efforts was the foundation for achieving real progress for Sugar. At the same time, it created an interesting tension as it diminished dependency on Sugar Labs central, potentially undermining the ability of the central organization to sustain itself.

- *A shared vision is essential, but visions evolve.* Many social enterprises are started by a small group of friends or colleagues who have a shared vision for how to change the world. Ensuring that this shared positive intention is translated into a clearly articulated vision for what the organization itself will focus on and how it will drive impact is vital. In the case of OLPC, profound differences of emphasis between the founders in particular, as well as other members of the founding OLPC team, ultimately drove the spin out of Sugar Labs and the eventual split of OLPC into the foundation and the association.

It is not unusual for irreconcilable differences to form between the founders of a social venture regarding the implementation of their vision. Nonetheless, as OLPC demonstrates, even after a split, it is possible to find ways to continue to work toward the original shared vision from different, complementary vantage points. Setting up a social enterprise to be a learning organization that can adapt to change is vital.

· *Drive global change while allowing for local innovation.* A small team with big ambitions cannot change the world by itself, but it can create a powerful foundation for change. Designing for viral adoption is fundamental to achieving scale while maintaining low overhead. By making intentions and outcomes clear, a disparate and distributed community can develop its own means toward a common goal. Any effort at fostering social change on a global scale must ensure clear articulation of those standards and best practices that will ensure consistency around those elements of a program that drive change. At the same time, room must be allotted for customization on the local or regional level. Many social-change organizations struggle to find the right balance between centralization and diffusion; in some cases, the central organization stifles innovation and contextualization, while in other cases lack of central control results in uneven quality and results that undermine the organization's brand and reputation.

PART 2

FROM IDEA TO IMPACT

FIVE

SELLING THE GREEN BANANA

"You know I don't do contracts, but what you do have is my word. And it's stronger than oak."

—Quarterback Matt Cushman's father committing
to representation by Jerry Maguire, just before
he signed a contract with a competitor

N HIS 2006 TED TALK, NEGROPONTE DREW A LINE IN THE SAND about the scope and scale of OLPC's bold ambitions for distributing computers: unless the organization had orders of 1 million laptops from each of five countries on at least three continents, production would not be started. "The days of pilot projects are over; when people say 'We'd like to do three or four thousand in our country to see how it works.' Go to the back of the line and someone else will do it, and then when you figure out that this works, you can join in as well."[1]

OLPC had been able to sell a vision of a soon-to-be-manufactured machine to five countries—Brazil, Argentina, Nigeria, Libya, and Thailand—each of which verbally committed to purchase 1 million computers (the minimum order). Many more world leaders—including Nguyen Tan Dung, the prime minister of Vietnam; Felipe Calderón, the president of Mexico; and Louis Michel, the European commissioner for development and humanitarian aid—were signaling their interest in working with OLPC. We had become an increasingly high-profile brand, and being associated with our program was a positive for leaders who wanted to impress upon their constituencies that education was a priority. Although we were encouraged by the attention we were getting, there was an increasing urgency to transform verbal commitments and non-binding memoranda of understanding into solid and enforceable contracts. The political value to heads of state, in most cases, could be realized in the photo opportunity and the subsequent public-relations uptick from being associated with OLPC. For us, however, a handshake was far from what mattered: getting laptops in the hands of children to drive learning.

In early 2007 OLPC had to solve two challenges: we needed to convert our most vocal fans (heads of state of developing countries and the leaders of multilateral organizations) into paying customers and, simultaneously, we needed to mold our messy blend of talent into an operating enterprise. Simply put, we had both sales and operations challenges.

On the sales side, our primary goal was to convert the multiple handshakes and letters of intent into cash-in-hand from at least one country to trigger the start of the assembly line. Operationally, we needed to land our first big contract and, from there, develop a sales strategy and business model that would allow us to both scale our operations and invest in the design of an even better and less expensive laptop. These challenges included (1) reconciling the needs of our for-profit production partners with those of our social mission in a way that would allow us both to meet our respective goals; (2) establishing financing partnerships with trustworthy financial-services organizations willing to issue letters of credit on behalf of developing-country governments; and (3) putting together a real sales capability that would go beyond handshakes. Building a sustainable business model while ensuring fidelity to a social mission is a conundrum familiar to every social entrepreneur. This chapter outlines the experiences of OLPC in reconciling these contradictory goals.

NO BIG DEAL

The technology landscape is littered with failed projects, products, and services that were good enough or even great in concept and capability, but failed to execute on a sustainable business model. In spite of all the media attention, design laurels, and social-impact recognition, the OLPC project was not immune to this phenomenon.

Although there was substantial promotion of OLPC from its start, it was not until late 2007 that the first concerted sales effort was put in place. Significant interest had been generated, public commitments had been made, and hands had been shaken, but not a single contract had been signed. When the "million-laptop minimum from five countries on three continents" ultimatum was repeated at an OLPC board meeting hosted by AMD in Austin, Texas, in February 2007, it was met, for the first time, with resistance from the board. After the meeting, former Dell Computer executive and Motorola board member Tom Meredith approached other board members to ask if we could reconsider these requirements. Meredith, saying aloud what much of the board felt, was afraid that setting the bar too high was distracting OLPC from addressing the hard work of creating partnerships and closing sales. The OLPC board, peopled by and large by representatives of association members, was deliberately designed to support the mission, not to critique its tactics; thus Meredith's concerns were not debated by the board at the time.

As it happened, Meredith's concerns were justified. As so often happens in the world of business, sales pipeline and backlog do not materialize into actual sales. This became our unfortunate reality. Countries found ways of delaying and then eventually walking away from the handshake commitments they had made. Presidents and ministers quietly backed off from highly publicized promises made to the media. The excuses included monetary shortfalls, lost budgets, political regime change, and changes to education priorities. At the same time, the competitive landscape was heating up. Potential competitors lobbied ministries of education, encouraging them to wait for their

---

COUNTING YOUR DEALS BEFORE THEY HATCH!

We probably had more confidence in our Thailand "handshake" than in any other deal. We had some remarkable results from pilot studies in schools run by the Thai royal family, and we also had a former MIT Media Lab PhD student, Roger Sipitakiat—currently on the faculty of Chiang Mai University—helping coordinate our efforts on the ground. Lastly, we had the support of Thaksin Shinawatra, the prime minister, who in 2006 had the funds in hand to pay for the program. But when Shinawatra was overthrown in a military coup, Thailand was not only no longer a done deal, it was no deal.

---

soon-to-be-released products, which they promised would meet the educational needs of a country with a more conventional approach and with the added benefit of being associated with established brands. After all, why buy from an unproven start-up non-profit organization when you can buy from a proven multinational corporation? Competition became a major challenge to closing deals and often led to delays in buying decisions. Our order backlog was quickly dwindling to zero.

Give One, Get One, and the $399 Laptop

Late 2007 was a time when we had a very favorable public image— thanks in large part to a press corps sympathetic to our mission—but from a business perspective, we had lost so much momentum that our very existence as an enterprise was at risk. It was in this context that the idea of "Give One, Get One" was born. Our hypotheses were that the US public had both the funds for and the interest in purchasing the XO laptop and that we could jump-start manufacturing by subsidizing laptops for children in the developing world through these US purchases. In the fourth quarter of 2007, we began to pitch a buy-two-get-one marketing campaign. For $399, anyone in the US could buy two XO laptops: one would be delivered to the buyer in the US, while the second laptop would be delivered to a child in the developing world. The offer made sense economically—since the price of the two XO laptops was still far less than the price of one commercial laptop—and it had the added benefit of being a tax-deductible contribution to a social mission. On top of this, T-Mobile donated one year of free WiFi access at any of its US hotspots to participants in the program. The Give One, Get One campaign was well-timed, as the media were still enamored with OLPC; their stories gave us marketing reach, helping to fuel our success. We also had the support of JCDecaux, the global outdoor-advertising giant, which donated billboard space across the country. Coordinating these promotion efforts were Larry Weber and his team at Racepoint Group, internationally recognized leaders in public relations.

The campaign was launched just prior to the 2007 Christmas holiday season. Our hope was that it would result in many hundreds of thousands of units sold, going a long way toward filling our order backlog. The results were mixed. On day one of the campaign, we broke records for PayPal sales (and, as it turned out, we sold roughly 50 percent of what would be our final total). Clearly there was a pent-up demand for the XO laptop. The OLPC program was off and running. Quanta could finally start building machines. All told, we sold roughly 180,000 computers—this was 90,000 distinct purchases with a total value of

---

EXPLOITING THE COMMERCIAL POTENTIAL OF THE LAPTOP

The success of the Give One, Get One program suggests that there was an unmet demand for low-cost laptop computers in the developed world. In late 2007, OLPC's technology was uniquely positioned to meet that demand, although the organization was not operationally capable of launching a global sales and distribution effort. We approached potential partners such as Dell, Lenovo, and Best Buy, but we were never able to close a deal—either because of a reluctance to cannibalize existing products, an unwillingness to take a risk on an unproven concept, or an inability to make the numbers work.

approximately US$35 million. For a for-profit technology company, this may not be a significant result; for a non-profit entity, however, touching the lives of 180,000 children in the space of two months is remarkable.

The significance of starting the manufacturing process with the Give One, Get One program should not be underestimated; it gave us new life and momentum. A short time after this program, Peru and Uruguay—both of which we had been speaking with for nearly two years—were able to see the final manufactured product. This gave them the confidence to solidify their deals with OLPC and place their orders; in the case of Uruguay, this resulted in a purchase of 100,000 computers. The Give One, Get One program produced the "seed sales" that provided us with our entrée into the marketplace. It made it possible to drive the launch of programs in Haiti, Rwanda, Ethiopia, Cambodia, Mongolia, and Afghanistan, and it also greatly broadened the community of participation in the project. We now had the product, the confidence, and the credibility to get in front of governments and talk to them, not just about our vision, but also about how our tangible product could help to enhance their country's educational system.

It should not be overlooked that the US economic environment in 2007 was robust; the Give One, Get One campaign benefited greatly from this positive economic period. One year later, we decided to re-launch the Give One, Get One program to an expanded audience, including Europe, with the tagline "Give a Laptop. Get a Laptop. Change the World." We again targeted the Christmas season, this time expanded the selling period to more than three months. We prepared advertising and marketing months in advance in order to enhance the execution of the program. A number of advertising firms volunteered their services pro bono, and a number of celebrities stepped forward to get involved in the project (including Masi Oka, Tom Brady, Mary Louise Parker, and even John Lennon posthumously, by agreement with Yoko Ono). In anticipation of large demand, we prebuilt a large stockpile of machines.

The factor we could not predict or plan for was the economic climate; in late 2008, Lehman Brothers, Bear Stearns, and AIG were all in the process of imploding: a significant financial crisis was setting in

WIN ONE, GIVE ONE

A little-known by-product of our expanded marketing initiative for the second Give One Get One program was that when a General Mills executive saw a billboard advertising our program, he came up with the idea of a "Win One, Give One Program" to be sponsored by General Mills. This campaign, launched in 2009, allowed more than 200 children in the United States to win an XO and give an additional XO to a child in Africa. General Mills wanted to promote social responsibility for children, and they thought OLPC was a great match. A significant marketing campaign supported the program and, in addition, General Mills has continued to provide funding to the OLPC project.

just at the time we launched our new initiative. The timing could not have been worse. People who had given freely one year earlier were now concerned about their jobs, their pensions, and the overall well-being of the global economy. In addition to tougher economic conditions, netbooks had made substantial inroads into the laptop market—the second Give One, Get One campaign was not conducted in a greenfield marketplace, but in one that was very competitive.

In spite of a much better executed Give One, Get One program with a great deal of marketing strength behind it—including full-length advertisements on the FOX network thanks to our supporter Newscorp—the program failed miserably: we sold less than one-tenth of the number of XOs that we had sold in 2007. The only thing that saved us was that we were able to sell the stockpiled machines to Peru. Without that sales outlet, we would have been finished, as we had outspent our cash on hand.

BALANCING MARGIN AND MISSION

In late 2006, OLPC brought on one of this book's authors, Charles Kane, to serve as chief financial officer, with the goal of guiding OLPC's transformation from focusing on innovation to focusing on production and deployment. Kane joined with a clear objective to help OLPC evolve from a handful of engineers into a more traditional enterprise, with all the financial and operational functions needed to support the realization of the mission. It was also imperative to create a revenue model to support the organization's long-term growth and sustainability. It was at the time of Kane's arrival that we began to debate the long-term strategy of the organization.

The Hard Realities of Price and Overhead

Kane observed that the OLPC project mirrored a typical start-up, just differing in terms of organizational structure and funding. In a for-profit start-up, growth and profitability are the measures of success. A non-profit measures its profitability in terms of the lives touched in meaningful and measurable ways. OLPC was trying to bridge the for-profit world—in which considerations of price and profit (in particular for our supply-chain partners) were essential—and the non-profit world—in which success is measured by lives touched. OLPC needed to translate a market typically defined by margins—maximizing the price customers were willing to bear—into one defined by volume. As a consequence, the internal logic at OLPC was different from that of a typical high-tech for-profit company: laptop *prices* needed to be as low as possible, and, while product features would be kept to a minimum, the product was required to meet the needs of children learning in harsh environments.

The need for a low-cost laptop was a hard constraint that severely limited our degrees of freedom both in financing our internal operational infrastructure and in negotiating with potential production partners. Unlike a for-profit company, which might have the option to increase price or to compromise on features in order to lower costs, we had very limited degrees of freedom. We could not increase price without putting the laptop out of reach of our target customer (and giving fuel to our vocal critics as we moved further away from the highly publicized $100 price tag). Likewise, we could not compromise on features without undercutting the potential of the laptop as a learning tool for children.

An additional constraint was simultaneously ensuring that we met our commitments to our supply-chain partners and realized sufficient margin on the laptops to finance the central OLPC organization. During the development phase of the project, we had financed our central operations from annual membership fees provided by members of our original funding coalition. Our run rate was relatively low as all our efforts were focused on engineering and design. However, as we transitioned to production and deployment, we anticipated growing to a point where membership fees would not be sufficient to cover costs. A small team could design the laptop, but a large team would be needed to deploy it.

The calculated bill of materials for the XO totaled US$187 per machine in 2007. The final (and publicized) price of the XO for government purchasers was $188 per machine, giving us a margin of $1 per machine (0.5 percent). We settled on the $1 margin after a simple back-of-the-envelope assessment: it should be adequate given our anticipated burn rate and the continuing assumption that we could sell 5 to 7 million machines each year. Taking just $1 also had marketing value, in particular when contrasted with the high margins charged for commercial laptops, whose high-margin, low-volume business model included margins of anywhere from 15 to 40 percent. We realized—but did not fully appreciate the significance of—the fact that the only way in which this razor-thin margin would be sufficient to cover overhead costs was if we were able to ensure demand for a lot of computers. Unlike typical manufacturing businesses, OLPC had no working capital; the key, then, was to creatively manage risk and cost to reassure our suppliers, maintain our own solvency, and satisfy the needs of our customers.

Solidifying the Supply Chain

The high-volume promise that would enable OLPC to self-fund our internal operations was both a constraint and a catalyst for solidifying our supply-chain partnerships. By 2007, OLPC had assembled a team of partners with much of the know-how and resources to go forward with mass production. Quanta—in partnership with AMD, Chi Mei, and Marvell—had signed on to manage the supply chain. These partners were enthusiastic about the OLPC mission, but they were unsure how to mesh their business practices with our social mission. OLPC had to build its partnerships based on a solid business model that ensured clear benefits to our partners in the near term and alignment of incentives to support sustainability over time. The challenge was reconciling margin and mission so that as OLPC grew, our partners would benefit as well.

The participation of each of OLPC's production partners was predicated on an assumption that they would make an upfront investment in support of OLPC as an advance against a promise of reliable (and significant) future profits. In some cases the up-front investment was a cash contribution, in others it was in-kind services to support product development or the establishment of the OLPC organization. For our largest partner, Quanta, it was physical construction of a new manufacturing plant specifically for the production of the XO outside of Shanghai. Given the size and significance of these up-front investments, OLPC was under pressure to deliver on its promise of high volume.

The bold promise of OLPC brought it to the attention of its supply-chain partners. However, as we got down to the details of production and delivery, there was a recognition that we were in a chicken-or-egg dilemma: in order to secure low costs with our production partners, we needed high volume; in order to achieve high volume, we needed low costs. It boiled down to the need to turn promises of orders into real orders. Not only would landing some orders demonstrate that OLPC had met the highly public promises; it would ensure that our partners realized a profit on their investment. Our chicken-or-egg dilemma predisposed OLPC to focus on high-volume sales rather than maximizing impact in the terms that ultimately mattered to us—education and learning. The dilemma also introduced some constraints that would limit the organization's ability to respond rapidly and fully to challenges and opportunities that emerged. For example, the perceived need for scale kept us from accepting deals that were anywhere from 5,000 to 50,000 XOs; they were simply not big enough to make business sense at the time. In retrospect (and even at the time) it is hard to consider multimillion-dollar deals as too small, but we left many such deals on the table.

In the end, sales were slower than expected, and the net overhead contribution from the $1 received from those sales we did close was not going to be adequate to cover our operating costs. In early 2008, the overhead rate was raised to $10 per machine (5 percent). There was no deep analysis that led to $10 per machine rather than the original $1 estimate. We just recognized the need to increase our margin and the fact that, to enable this, we needed to ask our purchasers to pay a bit more; this was a difficult task, not only given the much publicized $100 price point, but also the repeated promise that the price would never increase, only decrease, as sales volume increased. Separately, we pushed our supply-chain vendors to compromise a bit more on their margins. Once it became clear that the millions of machines in the backlog would never be converted to contracts, Quanta and Chi Mei effectively became vendors to OLPC. As OLPC received orders, we would go back to Quanta and Chi Mei to negotiate a specific unit price for each order. Quanta handled all the supply-chain management with the exception of the LCD screen, which was contracted similarly, but separately, from Chi Mei. Given that many of these companies were on our board, this was a fairly transparent conversation. Their vested interest in the success of OLPC provided the leverage needed to drive these compromises. Since many already had sufficient sunk costs associated with the project, they had further incentive to accept lower margins in order to ensure that OLPC had a future (and to increase the probability of recouping some of these sunk costs). Overall, the $10 margin was generally borne 60 percent by suppliers and 40 percent by customers, with some variability from deal to deal.

The $10 margin enabled us to cover our overhead and use any cash on hand to offer discounts on future sales to potential partners. Without the increase in margin, given the shortfall in sales volume relative to predictions, OLPC would have encountered difficulties in managing the additional costs associated with supporting deployments. Despite a business plan based on wishful thinking regarding sales volume, incomplete financial and business planning, and unexpected challenges, OLPC had worked its way into a structure that seemed to be sustainable.

FINANCING LARGE-SCALE SOCIAL CHANGE

Two topics that are currently being discussed by social entrepreneurs are the challenge of scaling their enterprises with limited working capital and the possibility of leveraging for-profit financial instruments to fund social change. In a very real sense, OLPC was wrestling with these questions as early as 2007 as we began to explore alternative means of ensuring the up-front availability of the millions of dollars needed for a developing country's government to purchase high volumes of XO laptops.

For a developing country, funding the minimum order of 1 million computers would require an outlay of US$188 million, which could represent a significant portion of their national budget. In a relatively wealthy country like Peru, this would represent 0.14 percent of the 2011 gross domestic product (GDP), whereas in Rwanda a purchase of this size would total more than 5 percent of the 2011 GDP. In most cases, the sheer amount of money required was likely to be prohibitive. On top of this challenge was the low likelihood of any government's being sufficiently convinced of the impact of an as-yet-unproven program to be willing to risk such a significant sum. For suppliers as well, the risk was substantial. A single shipment of one lot of XO computers (20,000 units) had a price tag of nearly $US4 million. For OLPC, a single payment default would have the potential to sink the OLPC organization financially. Considering these factors together, the success of OLPC required the creation of a capital market to mitigate risk for potential partner countries and supply-chain partners and for OLPC itself.

With this level of risk at play, our biggest partner, Quanta, insisted that each sovereign contract with a partner country have a letter of credit associated with it. In a traditional business transaction, the buyer gets an invoice and credit terms that state how the buyer will pay for the product; the standards tend to be payment upon receipt or up to ninety days post-delivery to pay required funds. In these cases, the seller is assuming the risk of loss if the buyer doesn't pay. Businesses have learned—often the hard way—that governments (and especially governments in developing countries) are particularly high risk. A change in political leadership can end a project and result in payment default; more commonly, a government will simply delay payments when it is running short on cash. Unlike the average person, whose credit rating is impacted by a failure to pay almost any kind of debt, the credit rating of a sovereign nation is based only on the repayment history for the bonds they issue and the strength of their central bank. Failure to pay a company for something they buy does not really hurt a government's bond rating, and therefore they behave accordingly. A letter of credit is a tool that mitigates this risk to ensure that a company gets paid.

OLPC and Citibank built the treasury services required to execute letters of credit. Citibank had previously identified OLPC as an organization whose mission aligned with the education and global impact initiatives of the bank's social responsibility programs. It had been looking for a way to support OLPC, and developing a treasury department to support sales was a perfect role. The bank's Global Trade Division volunteered its time and expertise to help OLPC ensure that a structure was in place to serve as a line of credit for our purchasers and to guarantee that our manufacturers would get paid when they delivered the laptops. It offered to help with the financial instruments and provision of the hundreds of million dollars of credit necessary to trigger physical production of the laptops. Citibank's openness to partnering with OLPC was essential to our success; it brought the global brand and presence in emerging markets that gave our supply-chain partners true confidence in the letters of credit that would be created. Citibank's global network of local banks—and deep reach into emerging markets—meant that it could leverage its existing relationships to solidify the letters of credit. We partnered with Citibank to develop a system to create letters of credit for any government buyer wanting to work with us. Without this financial structure, it is highly unlikely that we could have started production of the XO laptops. The letter of credit became our de facto capital sourcing. Citibank also brought a level of trust to the transaction that made everyone more comfortable; no longer were deals dependent on a small and unproven non-profit, but rather they

UNDERSTANDING LETTERS OF CREDIT

For OLPC, the letter of credit emerged quite quickly as the only clear means of effecting the partner government transactions to buy the high-volume lots of computers the organization was selling. The first letter of credit OLPC used was for Uruguay's purchase of 100,000 laptops (roughly US$18 million worth of computers). Uruguay had the money in hand to begin manufacturing, and it had binding government appropriations to cover the full cost of the computers; yet the vendors didn't want to begin production without a third party's committing to cover the costs if Uruguay failed to pay. Citibank's provision of a letter of credit cleared the way for the deal—one of OLPC's first—to get off the ground.

The letter of credit was both a blessing and a curse. While there was no risk in collecting payment when using a letter of credit as the vehicle of payment, it added a great deal of complexity to the sales process. Letters of credit take significant time and effort to create, and governments tend to be biased against them given the fees involved, which add to the overall cost of a deal. Once a letter of credit was solidified, every order had a built-in delay of at least three months (the time it takes to get parts, build the machines, and ship them). An additional "curse" was related to the painstaking process of executing a proper letter of credit. In many instances, the time delays and challenges of staging the proper initiation of the supply chain with the letter of credit led to deals either falling apart or being decreased significantly in size. However, we had no choice as our supply-chain providers made it crystal clear that a non-profit organization was in no way going to receive credit terms: letter of credit or no deal.

were backed by Citibank—supply-chain vendors and governments both had higher confidence that commitments would be honored.

DEVELOPING A SALES CYCLE

With supply-chain partnerships solidified and a mechanism for fronting and securing the large amounts of capital needed by partner countries to embark on an OLPC project secured, the next challenge was finalizing sales partnerships. After the failure to close on any of its initial deals, it became clear that OLPC needed to make the transition from a focus solely on mission and message to fielding a professional sales force that could close deals for million-machine commitments. There is an old English saying that defined OLPC: "Lions don't hunt mice." The public promises of the $100 price point along with volume commitments to supply-chain partners and the assumptions that the margins could be kept to $1 per year all hinged on our closing multiple deals, each for a million machines—OLPC had long roared like a lion, now it needed to hunt like a lion.

Kane's principal focus in his first year was building the systems and team to make this happen. He initially worked with two regional sales leaders: Latin America was in the hands of Rodrigo Arboleda (based in Miami and now the president of the OLPC Association), while Europe and Africa were covered by Walter De Brouwer (a serial entrepreneur who more recently has launched TEDxKids Brussels). The team focused on building a platform to track sales, established standard practices across the sales organization, and expanded the group to deepen relationships in key countries by recruiting salespeople with local expertise. The OLPC sales team focused on countries where they believed they could sell 1 million machines, and further focused on countries that showed interest through participation in the symposiums that the organization hosted at MIT. Salesforce.com contributed licenses to OLPC that allowed us to use its sales management platform and thus allowed the team to capture our sales pipeline in a disciplined approach. Operationally, we implemented weekly global conference calls and established a standardized sales pipeline to assess the true likelihood that a contract would be executed. At a strategic level, we began brainstorming innovative and bold ideas to jump-start sales of a large number of XO laptops. We stopped behaving like a "think tank" and starting employing proven business strategies.

The design of the OLPC sales force was typical of a modern technology company: with a pyramid structure that deployed a large sales force focused on tactical sales activities and multiple layers of management, with each successive layer covering a broader geography with an increasing focus on strategy. This pyramid structure is managed by a pipeline tool that tracks multiple objective measures of progress toward completed sales.

The challenge of applying this model to OLPC lay in the difficultly of establishing credible incremental measures of progress toward a contract; experience was teaching OLPC that contracts could become derailed at any time, and confidence in a deal's succeeding was very low right up until the documents were executed and money changed hands. This inability to predict the value of the sales pipeline wreaked havoc on the traditional sales-management approach, as managers couldn't effectively guide activities to focus the sales force in the field on opportunities that had the greatest potential to close.

SQUARING THE CIRCLE

As described above, since the time of its founding, OLPC has not always been a well-oiled machine. We have struggled to find our legs strategically, financially, and operationally. In the technology industry, most major companies specialize in either hardware, software, *or* services, and are successful in amassing hundreds of billions of dollars in valuation as "single thread" companies. OLPC, in contrast, addresses all three of these threads in our product delivery: we developed the XO hardware, we supply the Sugar software at no additional cost, and we provide support services (incomplete as they may be compared to all that is needed to fully support a large deployment). We had—and continue to have—only a small fraction of the employees needed to execute against the wide range of responsibilities we have taken on over time. What is very clear is that there was much we did not predict about the challenges ahead when we first outlined our vision and mission. We have been figuring it out as we go, dealing with a variety of unexpected internal and external factors. Some of the choices the organization made along the way—as well as the public promises that had already been made—made it unintentionally but significantly harder for OLPC to succeed.

And yet we have survived and prospered. Between 1999 and 2009, approximately 38,000 non-profit organizations (on average) were registered each year in the United States. Of these, only a handful, at most, will grow to national scale, and a large proportion will not be in existence in five years' time. In this field, there are only a handful of non-profits that have, to date, been as audacious and innovative as OLPC in attempting to bridge the for-profit and non-profit worlds to deliver a product, to take on an entrenched and arguably ineffective education establishment from a boldly different perspective, and to engage capital markets in new ways to enable social change. With more than 2.5 million XO laptops distributed to date, our financial results are quite remarkable: the annual revenue per employee for the average Fortune 500 technology company is roughly US$180,000. In contrast, for OLPC, it is roughly US$7 million—thirty-five times the industry average. Wall Street would be blown away.

LESSONS AND REFLECTIONS

- *All enterprises run on cash flow.* All the promises (and handshakes) in the world mean nothing if you do not have cash in the bank. Without cash, you do not have a business. So it is important to think ahead to what will make your business sustainable. Successful social entrepreneurs are good business people as well as visionaries. The technology landscape is littered with failed projects, products, and services that were good enough or even great in concept and capability, but failed to execute on a sustainable business model. You must balance margin and mission.

- *Keep your eyes open and believe what you see.* Every enterprise is influenced by external factors: changing economic conditions, changing social views, changing market forces from competitors. Singular focus on a visionary objective can expose the social enterprise to unforeseen risk and prevent the enterprise from capitalizing on evolving opportunities. Get out in front so that you can watch the landscape, anticipate change, and adapt. Base your strategic growth plan on the realities of market rather than wishful thinking or assumptions about what the market should do.

- *Only the adaptable survive.* To a large degree, the business challenges of our mission were more or less an afterthought. Any business, when it starts, tends to have broad goals and big ambitions. OLPC was no exception. But things rarely work out as expected. How an organization deals with change (in our case creating a business structure to secure the orders, creating the partnerships, and building laptops) is what makes it a business, not just another idea from academia. We made many mistakes along the way, but we have survived because we have been able to adapt, with our ultimate goal in our sights.

- *Organizational form will influence the choices available.* The decision to create OLPC as a non-profit enterprise had both positive and negative consequences. On the positive side, it meant that we were able to enter into partnerships where the terms were much more favorable than they would have been otherwise, as our partners were compelled by the mission: for example, the fact that Quanta covered virtually all the non-recurring engineering costs of developing the laptop and worked so tirelessly to manage the supply chain, keeping component costs low, is something that would only have happened in the context of a non-profit/for-profit alliance. It also meant that our customers—be they participants in Give One, Get One or heads of state—were (for the most part) more flexible and forgiving of long delay times between contract and delivery. On the down side, it meant that our access to capital was greatly restricted, since we don't have access to the traditional financial mechanism such as venture-capital funds or investment banks. In our case, this restricted access to capital made it much more difficult to expand to new markets and explore new ideas. As the market shifts to embrace more hybrid organizational forms (such as B Corps—organizations that uses the power of business to solve social and environmental problems), it may be that some of the constraints we faced are slowly lifting.

- *Sometimes "going slow in order to go fast" is the right approach.* In 2007 and 2008, OLPC got so caught up in selling laptops to Peru and Uruguay that it consumed all our energy and attention. We had no human resources or mindshare left to ensure that the laptops we were selling were being put to good use in the service of learning for children—our ultimate objective. Driven by the need to spark sales to sustain cash flow—and our organizational solvency—we lost sight of the very reason we had created our organization. Sometimes, replicating more slowly—and giving yourself the time to learn—is important.

SIX

FROM THE WAREHOUSE
TO THE SCHOOLHOUSE

*"The major reason for the lack of change in education is not due to lack
of ideas about learning on a micro or individual level, but rather is due
to a lack of models for growth and change at a macro or systemic level."*

—David Cavallo, Models for Growth

B Y LATE 2007 OLPC HAD FIGURED OUT HOW TO BUILD AND
sell laptops. With the help of Citibank, we were able to provide
the financing needed to manufacture laptops, and Quanta (our
Taiwanese manufacturing partner) was well positioned to manage
the costs of shipping, insurance, and freight to get the laptops from
the factory to ports of call in places such as Lima (Peru), Montevideo
(Uruguay), and Kigali (Rwanda). From there, conditions varied wildly.
OLPC's security guru Ivan Krstić, reporting from a warehouse in Lima,
sums up the situation we were facing:

Peru's first deployment module consisted of 40,000 laptops, to be deployed in
about 570 schools across jungles, mountains, plains, and with total variance
in electrical availability and uniformly no existing network infrastructure.
A number of the target schools are in places requiring multiple modes of
transportation to reach, and that are so remote that they're not even serviced

by the postal service. . . . Compared to dealing with this, the technical work
I do is vacation.

It is one thing to deliver laptops to a warehouse in Lima and another
to get the laptops into the hands of children in the Andes. In-country
logistics—getting the laptops into the hands of the children—would
become one of the biggest challenges of 2008.[1] After kicking off our
earliest deployments in 2007, we quickly realized the complications and
intricacies of fully supporting the deployment of the XOs and, perhaps
more importantly, integrating the technology into society. What came
much more slowly was an understanding of how OLPC could organize
itself to ensure, first, that the XOs made their way from the warehouse
to the schoolhouse and, second, that we were providing the necessary
supports to ensure that learning happened with the laptops.

As this book is written, OLPC has distributed more than 2.5 million laptops in more than 40 countries around the globe. This chapter
tells the story of how OLPC deployed these laptops. We describe how
we addressed logistical challenges, the various approaches we took to
teacher training and support, how we worked with our partners to increase the probability of learning happening with the laptops, and how
communities have become engaged. We describe our successes, but also
the mistakes we made along the way. Finally, we discuss our evolving
model of deployment and our "model for growth" for taking our program to scale.

From the beginning, OLPC had an efficient system for machine
distribution, albeit one that depended on the local client to hand-de-
liver the computers to each community. The OLPC laptop distribution
model was designed to ensure that machines that worked in local languages and were filled with software customized to the requirements
of the country were delivered into the hands of children. This was
accomplished in three parallel efforts. First, OLPC had a localization
process that created the language packages necessary for the software
to operate in the local language of the client and bundled specific content including textbooks, workbooks, and other templates. This image
was delivered to Quanta and was installed on each machine as it was

produced so that it would arrive in-country ready to distribute and use. Second, OLPC's security system generated activation keys on USB sticks that were designed to be delivered via a separate channel to the communities receiving the laptops. The laptops were useless until they were matched with the security key, and that did not happen until the machines had reached their intended recipient. Finally, the OLPC deployment model was designed to help clients estimate and plan for the level of effort required to physically deliver machines from a central warehouse to each community.

So long as the client committed to the physical delivery of the laptops to each community, and agreed to deliver the security keys to the laptop separately, the system was well designed to ensure that the machines were delivered to children ready to use. The diversity in capacity for dealing with these distribution issues, even within one region like Latin America, was extreme. While Peru and Uruguay each had ambitious goals and aggressive schedules for deployment (see Table 6.1), they had vastly different capacities for logistics. Krstić, upon returning from a visit to Peru, was dismayed to report that the Ministry of Education had, among other deficiencies, no inventory control system in place.[2] On the other hand, in Uruguay, the deployment was run by Laboratorio Tecnológico del Uruguay (LATU), an organization that straddled the public and private sectors and brought significant expertise in logistics that had been acquired through decades of coordinating nationwide infrastructure initiatives.

TABLE 6.1   AN AGGRESSIVE DEPLOYMENT SCHEDULE (LAPTOP DELIVERIES PER MONTH)

Date	Peru	Uruguay
February 2008	25,000	30,000
March 2008	15,000	12,500
April 2008		50,000

Our first step in supporting distribution was to write the *OLPC Deployment Guide*,[3] which detailed everything from the number of trucks needed to deliver laptops to the schools to the number of watt-hours of electrical service needed to power them. The *OLPC Deployment Guide* helped local program directors with the considerations for the different stages: planning, deployment, and operation. The general plan proposed was designed to be adapted for each new deployment according to a region's unique characteristics, context, strengths, and capabilities. It also provided a roadmap toward success: essential steps, decision points, and a timeline.

For the most part, we did manage to get the laptops from the warehouse to the schools. And, despite predictions of widespread theft, in three years' time less than one laptop in one thousand had been stolen (all when they reached communities, rather than in the distribution chain itself). However, a number of consistent barriers emerged once the laptops reached the towns and villages for which they were destined. A 2010 study by the Australian Council for Educational Research (ACER) of an OLPC pilot in the Solomon Islands—a sovereign state in Oceania consisting of nearly one thousand islands—illustrates the factors that consistently blocked computer usage there, as well as in many locations where the XOs were shipped.

- *Lack of power:* One of the most basic challenges encountered was lack or inconsistent availability of power. Of the three schools involved in the Solomon Islands pilot, only one had a generator to enable students to charge their laptops during the day. Students at the other schools had to go to the Distance Learning Centre—located quite far from their school—to charge their XOs.
- *Expense and difficulty of ensuring wireless Internet:* Additionally, to gain real advantage from the presence of the XOs, a school has to have satellite Internet capability in place; in the Solomon Islands, this was paid for during the initial pilot phase, but the school itself was unable to pay for connectivity thereafter. The result was that the program was phased out.

- *Technology breakdown and insufficient maintenance support:* In
  Niue, another of the three schools in the Solomon Islands, a
  school administrator indicated that despite some positive signs
  of impact on student motivation and learning, the program
  is being discontinued. They do not have local capability to
  troubleshoot and repair the XOs, nor do they have the funds to
  pay others to do so.

As in distribution of the laptops, Uruguay also did a good job addressing the challenge of Internet access; the necessity to ensure provision of access was baked into the deployment plan from day one, and LATU was tasked with developing a plan—successful, as it turns out—to enable universal access. Peru, in contrast, had similar aspirations, but the realities of geography conspired against their success. After three years of effort, a report from the World Bank indicates that less than 2 percent of schools have Internet. This lack of connectivity undercuts the potential power of the XO, for example by blocking the upgrading of software or preventing distribution of classroom materials.

By early 2008, even with the *OLPC Deployment Guide* in hand, it was apparent that some local distributions could succeed autonomously, while in many others, success would depend upon hands-on intervention by OLPC. There was still a huge gap between knowing what to do and actually doing it.

We saw a few options for supporting deployment in our partner countries. At one extreme was "drop and run"—simply ensuring that the agreed-upon number of laptops were delivered to the children. Success in this case would mean that the laptop and software survived transport and that OLPC did not take any additional responsibility for driving learning. Given our ultimate focus on learning for children, this was not an approach that we were comfortable supporting.

At the other extreme would be a "run the show" approach, in which OLPC would take responsibility for all aspects of distribution and deployment. OLPC aspired to operate on a global scale and to enable clear impact, but we were in no position to staff a logistics team in each market; this would require resources well beyond anything we would be able to assemble. Equally important, it was contrary to goals that were just beginning to be explicitly articulated for our deployments: that they be self-sustaining and build local capacity.

We landed, instead, in the gray area between these two poles. In this middle ground, our assumption was that, given OLPC's limited resources and our goals for project sustainability, as well as the fact that building a robust learning environment that incorporated technology would be hard work and would require significant time, there must be local ownership of the process of distribution and deployment, with OLPC providing guidance and tools.

ENSURING THAT LEARNING HAPPENED WITH THE LAPTOPS

Jonathan Nalder, mobile learning project officer for the Department of Education and Training in Queensland, describes his experience in providing computers for schools there: "As my own experiences over the last four years supporting technology deployments here in Australia have shown me, the initial stage of getting the hardware out to schools can be such a massive job, and the excitement of the students when it arrives so rewarding, that it's often easy to confuse this stage with what George Bush once called 'mission accomplished.'" As it would turn out, more challenging than distributing laptops to children in remote villages was ensuring that once the children had the laptops, they were used for learning. In the transition from distribution to operations, we had to determine how we could, with our limited resources, most effectively realize the goal that the laptops be used for "learning to learn."

Our first approach was to experiment with what we now call a "textbook deployment." Our assumption was that clients with the capacity to distribute textbooks to schools could utilize that same capacity to distribute laptops. This model depended upon the ministries of education taking the next step to integrate the laptop into their national curriculums. As with our original assumption that a handshake with a head of state would translate into laptop sales, this top-down deployment approach was often undermined by institutional inertia and lack of commitment. The second, and continually evolving, model

Children in Reaksmy, Cambodia with Panasonic Toughbooks™. (Photo by Nancy Seives)

The "Tunis" machine, a working prototype of the $100 Laptop jointly designed by the OLPC and Design Continuum teams, was presented at the 2006 World Summit on the Information Society Summit in Tunis, Tunisia, by Nicholas Negroponte and Kofi Annan. Mr. Annan broke the yellow crank—a symbol of OLPC's intention to build a hand-powered laptop—during the press conference. ©Continuum LLC 2006

A child from Nosy Komba, Madagascar, smiling after completing the Sugar Memorize game. ©Laura de Reynal 2012

Children in Uruguay commuting to school by horseback with their XO laptops (2007). OLPC Collection.

Children in Paraguay repairing XO laptops. ©2009 Bernardo Innocenti

Children in Ban Samka, Thailand, using the XO laptops to gather data © 2009 Barbara Barry

Seymour Papert in Senegal in 1982, pioneering one-to-one computing. ©Bob Mohl

Colombian soldiers distributing laptops in regions recently reclaimed from FARC. ©2009 Rodrigo Arboleda

depended upon community engagement. It was implemented and fostered by Carla Gómez Monroy, a long-time OLPC employee who had helped launch OLPC pilot programs in Nigeria, India, Mexico, Peru, Mongolia, Uruguay, and Paraguay. Her deployment model still depended on significant and coordinated support from a top-level national client. However, it sought to ensure that a parallel bottom-up approach of community engagement and training existed early on in any deployment, and it recognized that prolonged community effort and local ownership were key ingredients for success. Her rule of thumb was that she never told anyone what to do, but rather helped teachers and program administrators discover the potential of the laptop for education and, more importantly, the latent potential that was extant within their communities.

Gómez Monroy's approach was as much about community activation and engagement as it was about using computers. Her community engagement model involved developing a process for communities to both identify and solve challenges using the resources of the XO deployment. The result was that communities quickly achieved three critical successes: first, they were trained in the use of laptops; second, they were introduced to a process of community organization and problem solving; and, third, they were exposed to successes from the use of the XO to solve problems the community cared about fixing. While her model proved almost universally successful, the degree of success was dependent on having a leader to train and facilitate the community

GRASSROOTS DEPLOYMENT SUPPORT

Community deployment partners often came up with innovative solutions to problems they encountered that could then be used in other countries. In Paraguay, for example, the local deployment team wrote an inventory management system that could track the journey of every laptop from the warehouse to the classroom. This system is now in use in Peru, Nicaragua, and Rwanda, as well as a number of other countries.

learning process. The challenge for OLPC was how to scale this model and maximize the shared learning among our various communities.

AN OVERVIEW OF OLPC PROJECTS

In the appendices of this book, we provide detailed case studies of six of OLPC's deployments, chosen to provide the reader with an appreciation of the diversity of contexts in which we have deployed our program, the diversity of local impact ecosystems that have emerged, and the diversity of results to date. These case studies represent only a handful of the deployments that we have guided in over forty countries in regions including the United States, Latin America, Africa, Asia, Australia, and the Pacific Islands. The diversity of the OLPC deployments is virtually unprecedented in the world of technology and learning. The settings in which the deployments take place vary dramatically: How big is the country? How easy is it to travel and communicate between urban centers and rural areas? Do the target children live in an urban or rural setting? Do they live in poverty? How extreme? What other social-economic factors come into play? Have they had access to computing before? The list goes on.

Although societal and infrastructural characteristics may be obvious, a number of dimensions of diversity only become obvious when viewed from a slightly higher altitude, assessing the characteristics of the deployment rather than of the society in which the change is being initiated. As observed in a survey of OLPC deployments made by the Australian Council for Educational Research (ACER), "Current XO deployment projects vary in almost every respect, including how they are set up, funded, managed, implemented, and supported. All projects involve a number of entities, ranging from international donor agencies, national ministries or local departments of education and ICT companies, to non-government organizations or private non-profit foundations."

Lead Actor

Perhaps the most important factor that influences the evolution of a deployment in a partner country is the source of the original initiative and the breadth (or narrowness) of support that it enjoys within the country. We looked across the more than forty OLPC deployments to date and sorted them into five broad categories: (1) those begun by initiative from the executive branch of the central government; (2) those in which the Ministry of Education played the primary role; (3) those driven by private sector initiative; (4) small, generally local, NGO-led initiatives; and (5) those, also typically local in scale, that were started through the initiative of a member of the community.

In Rwanda, for example, the project is driven by President Paul Kagame and linked to a broader agenda of social and economic development and post-war reconciliation. Although the Ministry of Education plays a lead role in implementation, given the small size of the country and its current status as a benevolent dictatorship, the project is both tightly controlled by the center and has the benefit of the full set of governmental resources to draw on. Likewise in Uruguay, OLPC represents to President Tabaré Vázquez an opportunity to "increase connectivity and reduce the digital divide"; it is one of the planks of an initiative to realize a greater level of social equality in the country and to broaden opportunities for its citizens (since Vázquez is a physician, he often uses an analogy to vaccination to illustrate his point). In Peru, a member of the Ministry of Education, Oscar Becerra, led the OLPC charge, and spent significant resources building buy-in from a broader set of governmental stakeholders to ensure that the necessary resources could be brought to bear in support of the project. As the history of this deployment has shown, he was wildly successful in doing so, and Peru can, in many ways, be held up as the poster child of balance between top-down and bottom-up initiative in support of instituting technology for education.

One risk of having your project attached to a head of state is the risk of political instability. In Thailand and Pakistan, for example, politics intervened and sidelined the project, when prime ministers Thaksin Shinawatra and Pervez Musharraf, respectively, were deposed and sent into exile. On the flip side, one clear measure of success is surviving a regime change. In those three cases where we deployed through a presidential initiative—Peru, Uruguay, and Rwanda—we have outlasted the administrations that initiated the original deployment: José

"Pepe" Mujica has kept the Vázquez program intact in Uruguay, Ollanta Humala has changed some of the priorities, but is continuing Alan García Pérez's program in Peru, and the Kagame administration is still in power in Rwanda and has consistently articulated strong commitment to the project.

A non-governmental, local champion for OLPC is becoming the new norm in successful programs. In Paraguay, the initiative has been driven from the ground up by Cecilia Rodriguez Alcalá, founder and director of a small NGO, Paraguay Educa. The scope and articulated focus of the initiative have been less grand and far-reaching than in government-led programs: her goal is to change the country for the better by putting 20,000 laptops into the hands of children and focusing on building in them the new skills that she believes are "fundamental for the creation of development." Similarly, the OLPC program managed by the family foundation of María Josefina Terán de Zamora and Roberto Zamora Llánes epitomizes how the private sector can drive huge impact. Through a public-private partnership, the Zamoras have provided laptops to more than 25,000 kids; similar partnerships are emerging in Colombia and South Africa.

There are numerous lessons to be drawn from the contrast between these centrally driven projects and smaller grassroots efforts. First, the path may be longer and more difficult since a president can use the bully pulpit to tell the OLPC story and sway public opinion, while a small NGO can only show the way and hope that others will follow. Second, the original scale of the initiative is necessarily much more limited, as the extent of resources and the ability to influence the variety of actors needed is much more circumscribed for the NGOs. However, the initial size of the deployment does not seem to figure into how successful it will be over time. Our original assumption that only a large-scale deployment would attract the critical mass of interest and talent to build something sustainable was not correct. While some of the deployments were certainly large scale, smaller deployments have been key to the growth of the program, not just in terms of numbers, but also in terms of developing the environment for future growth.

What has become clear over time is that a small deployment such as Paraguay or Nicaragua can be viable if there is both leadership and

OLPC AUSTRALIA

Rangan Srikhanta had heard about the OLPC project even before taking a job with Deloitte in Australia. For a while, he managed to juggle his day job and his passion for the project: "I'd sneak out of work at lunch and ship laptops to Fiji and Samoa." His desire to bring the program to the aboriginal children of Australia eventually led him to leave his job at Deloitte in order to work full time on what became OLPC Australia. He raised funding through donations from major Australian corporations resulting in the roll out of thousands of computers, coupled with a training support program. This led to the recent order of an additional 50,000 computers by the Australian government and a long-term commitment to enhance the educational system of its poorest communities.

community engagement. Further, because small deployments necessarily need to rely on resources developed elsewhere, they don't tend to fall into the "not-invented-here" trap and thus are more open to adopting and adapting best practices from wherever they arise. This is not an easy arrangement for OLPC, as these deployments need a disproportionate amount of attention, but they are our most powerful marketing tool.

Social Change Agenda

Another key factor that influences the evolution of a deployment is the social change agenda, in particular whether the focus is on improving the school system or driving learning for children. These two agendas are farther apart than they may seem at first blush: while improving the school system generally focuses on showing measurable increases in standard measures of knowledge acquisition and skill (reading, writing, and arithmetic), driving learning often has a more aspirational focus on building life skills that will enable children to transform their realities and leaves more room for innovation, experimentation, and community engagement. Typically, although not always, a more centrally driven initiative will default to a focus on the formal school system,

PLAN COLOMBIA REVISITED

In 1999, Colombian president Andres Pastrana launched "Plan Colombia," a set of social development projects to help alleviate the tension between the left- and right-wing militants at odds with the central government. With US funding and involvement, the program put its focus on curbing drug smuggling and combating the left-wing insurgency. It was in that context that Rodrigo Arboleda, Nicholas Negroponte, and Walter Bender approached USAID with a proposal to deploy one-to-one computing in the barrios reclaimed by the military: i.e., turning swords into laptops. We were rebuffed at the time, so it was especially satisfying one decade later to be able to deliver, through the Colombian military, XO computers to the children of former insurgents.

while a grassroots initiative tends to have a greater focus on driving learning and broadening life opportunities for children.

Where the commitment by the lead actor—whether governmental, NGO, or private sector—to the program in general and to the learning agenda in particular runs deep, the program generally proceeds well. Where the commitment is little more than a public relations campaign, we have faltered. In some cases, such as the early deployments in Mexico, machines were distributed as part of a plan for making technology more broadly available to children, with no regard to the OLPC principles of deployment and similarly no regard for local appropriation. In such cases, while there was a very genuine commitment to helping improve the lives of children, there was not a corresponding commitment to the pedagogical model for which the XO and Sugar were developed. We do not consider these initiatives successful.

Looking across the range of our deployments, we see an additional dimension of the social change agenda that emerges: the degree of focus on driving social inclusion and enhancing social equality. Oftentimes, the proxy for this is the choice between a deployment in an urban center versus a deployment that encompasses, or focuses solely on, rural areas. In most of the developing world, living in an urban setting is by no means a guarantee of a quality education; however, living in a rural setting almost always guarantees poor education, if any. Except in circumstances where saturation could conceivably be achieved—as in a small country like Uruguay—deployments have tended to focus on rural (or semi-rural) populations first. And even in Uruguay, the sequence was to first saturate the countryside and then deploy in the capital of Montevideo. In Peru, the priority placed on reaching the rural areas was a key driver for, and hallmark of, the program. The advantage of this approach, above and beyond reaching the neediest population, is that saturation is relatively easy to achieve. The disadvantage, of course, is the difficulty of bringing laptops, electricity, and the Internet to remote locations and the burden placed on ongoing support and training. Nonetheless, whether for political or other reasons, governments and NGOs have overwhelmingly targeted rural populations.

Holistic or Siloed Efforts

Some deployments have taken a holistic approach, tackling everything from logistics to pedagogy within the context of one organization. Others have built silos around different components of the deployment, with the Ministry of Telecommunications worrying about connectivity, the Ministry of Finance worrying about the budget and electrification, and the Ministry of Education worrying about content.

Perhaps the best example of a holistic approach that can serve as a guidepost for the various things that must be in place to support the success of a program comes from the NGO-led efforts of Paraguay Educa, which developed expertise in logistics, pedagogy, and marketing, all coupled with strong and focused management. They are autonomous from the government, thus free from the day-to-day whims of the political system; they have a close relationship with several top-notch engineering universities from which they can draw upon expertise and interns; they are dedicated to delivering a service at a high quality; and they have a strong leader with a clear vision of the overall project. Most importantly, they built infrastructure well in advance of need. From the beginning, they put an emphasis on building partnerships, building a strong technical team, and building a strong pedagogical team—in each case, investments that were outsized relative to the immediate needs of their initial deployment. The result, however, is that they are in a position not only to scale, but to drive clear impact and serve as a reference point for others.

In Uruguay, in contrast, the project has been driven in large part by a technical team responsible for providing universal Internet access. As a result, the pedagogical program has, until quite recently, been significantly less well developed. That said, there have been wonderful contributions made at a grassroots level by individual teachers and community volunteers that have set a foundation on which the pedagogical efforts can build. In Peru, the ministry has focused on pedagogy, producing some excellent guides for teachers. However, it has been unable to solve the puzzle of connectivity in rural areas and as yet has not found a partner who can help them do so. It also failed until recently to engage local governments in taking an active role in the program. This lack of a holistic approach has led to significant criticism of the program and accounts, to some degree, for the relatively slow progress in Peru versus that of some of its neighbors.

What we can say by looking across our deployments is that the ability for an OLPC project to evolve from a pilot program to a social movement is a function of three things: (1) the breadth and appeal of the vision; (2) the amount and consistency of support and resources (political, social, financial, and human) available to realize the vision; and (3) the depth of commitment to the desired impact.

CREATION OF AN IMPACT ECOSYSTEM

In his paper "Models for Growth," David Cavallo described the pitfalls of the "replicate and scale" model, where a fully conceived change is imposed from the top down in a hierarchical fashion, only to be rejected by those being force fed. He also pans the small pilot model, which rarely achieves any meaningful scale. While, on the surface, our approach at OLPC seems to be top-down—distributing laptops from a central point, the use of the laptops is not predetermined. Rather, their use is intended to be emergent, with the extent and type of impact very much a by-product of teachers, children, and their parents learning together, discovering new possibilities, and sharing those discoveries. While we have, until very recently, been largely agnostic about curricula—with the noted exception of an insistence that every child learn to program a computer—we are not agnostic about learning. We encouraged deployments to create what Cavallo would describe as "environments for growth" that, among other things, broadened the sense of possibility, provided new tools, enabled local initiative, and supported experiential learning.[4]

Despite the rich diversity of OLPC deployments to date, it is very important to note that in each case of a successful deployment, an ecosystem emerged that included a cross-sector group of actors from the public, private, and non-profit sectors and embodied many of the characteristics that Cavallo noted. In our successful deployments, these "impact ecosystems"—although perhaps in a different manner and sequence—addressed three fundamental barriers that stood in the way of realizing the promise of technology in driving learning for children: (1) supporting teacher adoption; (2) addressing curriculum integration; and (3) helping to more fully realize the earlier promise of Gómez Monroy's model of community engagement.

Teacher Training

Few if any teachers in developing country classrooms have experience integrating computers into their teaching. A cynical but realistic Negroponte captured the situation well: "[W]hen you go to these rural schools, the teacher can be very well meaning, but the teacher might only have a sixth-grade education. In some countries, as many as one-third of the teachers never show up at school."[5] While the situation in many OLPC countries is not nearly as bleak as what Negroponte describes, it is certainly the case that teachers are often under-prepared to effectively play their roles and default to rote methods of teaching that are less conducive to integration with technology. Many teachers, upon hearing about the program, were reflexively defensive: being a teacher is often a high-status position in developing countries, and many of them felt that the computers would undermine their authority in the classroom by giving students alternative sources of information and knowledge. Likewise, many felt uncertain how to appear confident and in charge at the front of the class while using a tool that with which they were not comfortable. That the XOs would have a positive impact in the classroom under these conditions was not a given.

OLPC faced a challenge of how to train teachers in a way that would both meet the conventional expectations of government and educational stakeholders and have an impact on the culture of learning as articulated by Papert. It was necessary that we work with deployments to develop training workshops for teachers that were designed to take them from a very humble and traditional starting point (instructors providing rote education in most cases) to being able to mentor students engaged in the authentic problem solving that characterized constructionist learning. As expected, there were some maverick teachers in every country who were quickly able to exploit the laptops to their fullest, leading the way for others. And there were—and are—teachers who are slow to pick up the technology or stray from a set curriculum.

In general, teacher training in OLPC deployment countries was, in our first deployments, minimal at best. It quickly became obvious that, given that the computers were primarily sold through formal institutional channels for use in schools, building the buy-in and capabilities of the teachers was vital. Equally as obvious was that, despite our hopes, the "textbook" deployment model would never take off; this meant that ministries of education tended to approach OLPC projects with little expectation that they should chart a path for teachers to learn how to use the laptops, let alone learn how to integrate them into their classroom teaching. OLPC would need to step in to help to fill the gap.

Curriculum Integration

Another barrier that consistently emerged—and that various actors in the ecosystem would collaborate to address—was the need to help

---

AN UNEXPECTED OFFSHOOT OF OLPC

In OLPC projects around the world, children and their teachers have often used our new technology by being creative and starting new businesses. This trend is particularly notable in Uruguay, where students have written dozens of Sugar activities. Christofer Yael Roibal Perez an early user, is now emerging as a gifted software developer. Roibal, who is from a small town northeast of Montevideo, has begun modifying Sugar itself. He recently started using Unity, the new desktop on Ubuntu GNU/Linux systems; while he liked it, he missed some of his favorite Sugar features so he began to build his own "mash-up" between the two systems. Children like Christofer, confident in their ability to actively solve problems, are the future leaders of their countries.

---

teachers and school administrators connect the XOs and their activities to the formal school curriculum. As part of our formal and informal deployment support, OLPC has attempted to facilitate the emergence of standards for how to linking the technology to the curriculum. Additionally, we have tried to influence the learning environment to ensure that the vital "informal" time with computers was either baked into the school day or enabled in another manner. For example, in Peru, teachers are provided with guides to Sugar-inspired, project-based learning activities that can supplement the standard curriculum. In Paraguay, in contrast, there has been an emphasis on using the laptop during informal time; there are many children who attend Saturday sessions that are dedicated to the creative uses of the computer. In Rwanda, informal time is built into the school day, since the government has yet to agree to let the computers go home with the children due to safety concerns.

In summing up what she had learned by guiding so many of OLPC's pilots over the years, Gómez Monroy crafted a set of brief verses to capture the essence of the lessons for others following in her footsteps:

The Child
- Children's natural hands-on curiosity is their best teacher.

- Let them explore.
- Give them time.

The Teacher

- There's a child in every teacher.
- Let yourself explore.
- Give yourself time.

The Implementer

- There's a teacher in every child.
- Regard child, teacher, and community.
- Learn from them, model for them.

LESSONS AND REFLECTIONS

In a 2006 article on One Laptop per Child in *Technology Review*, James Surowiecki made a dramatic pronouncement:

> OLPC will, should it succeed, serve as a new model for getting the nonprofit, private, and public sectors to work together efficiently and productively. . . . [T]here are problems too big to be solved by NGOs or corporations (or governments, for that matter)—problems that demand new kinds of alliances. OLPC is, in that sense, not just building a new computing machine. It's also building a new philanthropic machine, one as cobbled together and untraditional as the $100 laptop. The question that remains is just how well either of those machines will really work.

Surowiecki underscored his pronouncement by explaining that, not only were we trying to "create a project of vast scale and scope," but we were doing so "on a budget that is, even by philanthropic standards, surprisingly small." What follows are a few of the lessons we feel we have learned from this diversity of experience.

- *One size doesn't fit all.* Conditions for deployments vary widely, and each project should be carefully planned for success in the unique conditions of that town, region, or country. This includes setting up a "scouting period" for each deployment, in which the project team can identify existing local resources that can be leveraged to support success. For example, in Uruguay, this meant leveraging the in in-place regional distribution centers as hubs for laptop distribution. (It is also vital that you identify key gaps in local resources and develop a phased plan to fill those gaps.) Leveraging existing resources can drive greater efficiency and sustainability of a deployment, as well as increase the degree of community buy-in and participation.

- *There are no shortcuts.* Our initial focus on distribution of the XOs as the end goal, and the perception of some of our country partners that the XO was, itself, an end-to-end solution, has resulted in some deployments underestimating the time and resources necessary to create a successful intervention. What has become clear to us over time is that a deployment needs to consider the entire learning ecosystem, of which the laptops are only one part. OLPC works with deployments to create the entirety of the ecosystem, but it is necessarily hard work—it should not be underestimated. A coalition needs to be built to cover all the needs of a deployment. For any social entrepreneur, ensuring that you're clear on the totality of necessary supports for impact—either providing them yourself or ensuring they are provided in another manner—is vital.

- *Learn from (the mistakes of) others.* The global community has lots to offer in sharing best (and worst) practices. For OLPC, those deployments that tried to operate in isolation often repeated the mistakes of others and got stalled on trivialities. Those deployments that reached out to the global community made rapid progress and got an additional boost from the feeling of connection to a larger purpose. The analog for most social enterprises is finding a way for your sites to connect with and learn from one another.

- *Your success is ultimately dependent upon what others do, not just what you do.* In Peru and Uruguay, OLPC got everything we had wished for—countries that fully embraced the one laptop per child concept. It was clear to us that the success or failure of these two launch countries would be critical to the long-term success of OLPC, and although our unspoken commitment was that we would do everything that it took to ensure success, it was largely out of our hands. Only commit to what you can control, and prepare contingency plans for those things you cannot control.

- *Build local capacity.* Even if it is not the short path to success or the most immediately efficient, local capacity is necessary for long-term sustainability. OLPC began to focus consistently on local capacity building, i.e., teaching local OLPC staff and partners how to manage their projects and helping them to develop the resources they would need to be successful over time. You cannot do everything yourself if you want to be a global enterprise.

SEVEN

NEITHER MAGIC NOR FAST

ASSESSING THE IMPACT OF OLPC

*"I have not met anybody who claims they are too poor to invest in educa-
tion, nor anybody that said it was a waste of money. If somebody is dying
of hunger, food comes first. If somebody is dying from war, peace comes
first. But if the world is going to be a better place, the tools for doing so
always include education."*

—Nicholas Negroponte

*"Why is it people only question investing in ICT [information and
communications technology] when it goes to poor children while every
wealthy school makes it widely available with no argument or struggle
against?"*

—Jose Antonio Chang, former Peruvian minister of education

N A DECEMBER 6, 2010, ADDRESS, PRESIDENT OBAMA CITED
the United States' poor and declining performance on the Program
for International Student Assessment (PISA)—a seventy-country assessment of relative educational performance—as evidence of dimin-
ishing future economic prospects. In Obama's view, the PISA results

showed that the United States was in another "Sputnik moment." Just as in 1957, when the Soviet Union beat the United States into space and sparked a societal push to advance in science, technology, and education, our current declining educational performance should, in his view, serve as a wake-up call to invest ourselves again in innovation and education.[1] Education, he stated, was the platform on which a nation's economy is built and the fundamental prerequisite to innovation.

Although there seems to be a general consensus that a well-functioning educational system and well-educated young people are the foundation upon which societal well-being is built, educational reformers in the United States and on the international stage have struggled for decades to define what "success" in education looks like. Some focus on the experience of students and the characteristics of schools: Are students calm, rested, and sufficiently well fed to concentrate on their studies? Are they studying in safe, well-resourced schools? And are they taught by qualified, high-performing teachers who stay on the job? In school systems that are low performing, do we see clear progress against defined school-improvement plans that address key conditions blocking student success? For others, it is obvious that we must look beyond these contextual indicators toward measures of outcomes, but it is not clear which outcomes really matter: Should we be looking for higher standardized-test scores, lower dropout rates, a larger proportion of high school graduates, a larger number of students from all backgrounds attending college, higher college graduation rates, job readiness, or some other measure of impact?

Implicit in President Obama's "Sputnik" perspective is potentially a very different definition of success, which focuses less on education and more on learning; less on the student, more on the learner. In this view, educational success is about providing our youth with the skills, mindsets, and capabilities that they need to survive and thrive in the world. The focus is the development of creativity, innovative capability, critical thinking, and problem-solving skills as the key metrics of success.

OLPC has tried to focus, in our work, on measurable impact on individual learners and on the culture of learning in those countries with which we work. Our history of deploying laptops in partnership with governments means that we've had to find a way to speak to those who focus on more traditional measures of "school effectiveness." And yet, our own roots are in constructivist learning theory and Freire's revolutionary educational ideology, which focus much more on the abilities of the individual learners and the extent to which they become empowered as change agents in their own lives and societies. This has often been an uneasy truce in discussions about impact. Perhaps our greatest challenge over the years has been making the outcomes of our program visible and understandable to the variety of stakeholders involved.

HARD TO DEFINE, HARDER TO MEASURE

For a project that has touched the lives of as many children as OLPC, it is hard to point to incontrovertible evidence of impact. The raw data tracking our activities to date are impressive: OLPC has delivered XO laptops to more than 2.5 million children in hundreds of cities and towns in more than forty countries. Sugar software (including the version embedded in the XO computer, Sugar on a Stick, and the downloadable version) is in use by many millions of children and teachers. We have raised US$50 million in revenue to date from philanthropy, and an additional US$500 million in revenue from laptop sales. Dozens of countries have already contracted to buy millions of computers for distribution in developing-world contexts for 2012.

However, there are clear limits to a "counting" approach to measuring success. We can measure the number of laptops delivered to children, but that doesn't tell us very much about how the laptops were used. We can tally the number of hours the laptops were used and even log the activities that the children use, but there is not a simple mapping between using a computer and learning with a computer. We can subject children to standardized tests, but these tests tend to measure what children know, not what they can *do* with that knowledge. In other words, it is relatively easy to aggregate data, but very hard to come up with a measure of impact.

That OLPC has encountered difficulty in measuring our impact is not, despite the enormous amount of attention this has received, very

remarkable when viewed against the broader backdrop of social programs. As the Coalition for Evidence-Based Policy says, "In most areas
of social policy—such as education, poverty reduction and crime reduction—[programs] are often implemented with little regard to evidence."[2] However, the fact that we are not remarkable in this regard is
not an excuse. We did not deliberately drop the ball on evaluation, but
as it turns out, our original approach was inadequate.

In 2007, as we launched in Uruguay and Peru, Bender and David
Cavallo created an Evaluation Framework to serve as a guide for all
OLPC deployments. Our assumption was that providing a structured
framework for evaluation would enable the network of funders, universities, and program managers in our partner countries to begin to
gather data in a consistent way. We assumed that every project would
take the Evaluation Framework and eagerly engage in assessment of impact, in large part because the agencies that purchased the XOs would
be held responsible for demonstrating impact to their funders.

However, the reality on the ground is that evaluation has been
conducted in an inconsistent manner across the hundreds of OLPC
deployments. To our surprise, evaluation was not always a high priority with many of our clients. There was tremendous pressure from
governments to deploy the laptops they had purchased quickly, which
meant the XOs were often distributed before an evaluation plan could
be put in place. Another common, but unanticipated reason for not
prioritizing evaluation was the fear expressed by some clients that if the
XOs did not deliver clear impact, this would indicate that the government had wasted money. As it turned out, one of the limitations of our
decentralized and locally owned approach to deployment was a lack
of rigor regarding standards for evaluation. The result is that for many
deployments, evaluation is lacking; for others, data are incomplete or
of poor quality.[3]

Another limitation to impact assessment is that each of our deployments is highly customized based on the resources, motivation, and
characteristics of the local context. As observed in a survey of OLPC
deployments made by the Australian Council for Educational Research (ACER), "Current XO deployment projects vary in almost every

respect, including how they are set up, funded, managed, implemented, and supported. All projects involve a number of entities, ranging from international donor agencies, national ministries, or local departments of education and ICT companies, to non-government organizations or private non-profit foundations." ACER concludes that "different stakeholder groups hold different expectations of the program and not all evaluations are necessarily focused on measuring educational outcomes." The result is that it is hard to extrapolate what, beyond the presence of an XO with Sugar embedded in it available for each target child, is consistent across all OLPC's deployments. Evaluating impact of projects this diverse is difficult, if not impossible. As it stands, if you believe in our approach, there are data to support your view; if you want to show that we're coming up short, you can find anecdotal data to support that position as well.

EVALUATING IMPACT ON STUDENTS

The original OLPC Evaluation Framework was meant to reinforce a shift from focusing on knowledge acquisition as measured by standardized testing[4] to a focus on assessing the skills that students acquired and, in particular, whether we saw evidence that they were "learning to learn." For students, the framework included their behavior in the school context, including attendance, grade repetition, and dropout rates. It also incorporated specific information about access to technology and usage of technology ranging from the amount of in-class and out-of-class time with the computer to more sophisticated measures of how students were using the computer. Were they using it to play games, chat with one another, or create new programs? Impact on students was measured within the bounds of technological fluency, acquisition of traditional classroom skills (literacy, mathematics, and communication), and measures of non-traditional skills that correlated directly to constructionist learning theory, such as creative thinking, problem-solving abilities, collaboration, teamwork and self-guided learning.[5] Beyond these measures of behaviors, knowledge, and skills, the framework also pointed to a chain of impact from motivation to acquisition of knowledge and skills, and subsequently expanded sense of confidence and self-efficacy.

The challenge, and the opportunity, then, is to look across the partial evidence from our various deployments to each of the linkages in this chain of impact that moves from student access to and usage of computers to motivation, learning, capability building, and the expansion of possibilities for their lives.

Student Motivation for Learning

In a posting to a mailing list for Pacific educators, Brian Bird, the principal at Patukae, one of the three schools involved in the 2008 OLPC pilot in the Solomon Islands, stated his clear opinion of the impact of OLPC: "While it is true that technology is not in itself responsible for driving change, it is a tool that can be used to drive change in learning and commitment to learn."[6] Experiences in other locations reinforce this message. A study conducted in 2009 in Peru by the Inter-American Development Bank (IADB)[7] noted that 95 percent of the teachers in schools that received the laptops think that they contribute to improving the children's education and learning, and that this motivates them to attend school. In the Solomon Islands, teachers noted that students reacted positively to the novelty of the laptops and were consistently excited by the possibility of using them to learn new things.

The uptick in motivation and sense of possibility that the XOs may generate (even if short-term) also manifests in a shift in school-related behaviors. In Nicaragua, for example, over the course of two years, schools in which XOs have been distributed show a decline of 50 percent in the dropout rate and a similar reduction in the number of students repeating grades. In Rwanda, as well, school data indicate a measurable reduction in students missing class and increased student engagement in seeking information for schoolwork.

One of the most consistently reported—and hardest to measure—areas of impact of OLPC may be in regard to the sense of confidence and self-worth that receipt of the laptops imparts to children. In a survey conducted by the director general of education technology

A NEW CONFIDENCE GAINED IN URUGUAY

Rosamel Ramírez, a teacher, tells the story of "Pedro," a fourteen-year-old boy in her class who didn't know how to read and who had serious behavioral and social problems. When the XO laptops arrived, Rosamel suggested that each student compose a story of their own choosing. Pedro wanted to write about a character he recently discovered from a play: "Teacher, I want to write about Nacho . . . but I don't know how." Rosamel coached Pedro to tell her the story out loud, and then helped him write his story phonetically on the XO, word by word. Pedro knew almost all of the phonetics, but not how to spell nor how to join the words. Rosamel said: "What beautiful work you did! Now you have to read it to your classmates." He responded, "But I don't know how to read." With a wink she responded, "Ah, it doesn't matter, you will know because this is your story." He read it many times in silence and then stood in front of the class and read it to his classmates. At the end, he shouted excitedly, "I know how to read, I know how to read!" For Pedro it was an unforgettable day. –Rosamel Norma Ramírez Mendez, sixth-grade teacher in Uruguay. Translated from the original Spanish by Gabriel Eirea.

(DIGETE) in Peru, it was found that students in OLPC programs had an increased interest in school (an 11 percent increase relative to their peers without XOs) and that these same students showed a substantial increase in the importance they ascribed to attending school. Their sense of competency in school increased. Perhaps most importantly, 50 percent of student respondents reported that they had a sense that they now had choices in life.

XO Usage by Students

In looking at usage of the XOs, there are some important dimensions to consider: frequency and amount of use; the balance of formal time with informal time; and usage both at school and at home. An additional dimension is what students do with their XOs; are they engaged in word processing, game playing, or potentially more creative, individually-defined endeavors?

Frequency of Usage

The ACER report in the Solomon Islands stated that students used their XO laptops "every day that they are charged," both in school and at home. Our original hypothesis was that, contrary to most ICT for education programs, which emphasized structured, in-school time, it was in the informal time that the greatest creative learning would happen; with this in mind, access both in school and at home is vital.

Proponents of home use argue that this provides children with more informal time with the computer and is therefore likely to support the type of use of computers that promotes creativity and problem-solving capability. Critics argue, in contrast, that children will spend the time on the computer playing games or engaging in other learning-lite activities, time that they could better spend working, playing outside, or interacting with family and friends. The IADB study in Peru reported that 80 percent of students took the computers home. When they did so, they tended to use them for an additional one to two hours, about half of which was for school work and the other half for recreation such as playing games or chatting with friends.[8] Across the board, there is a sense that the XO has the potential to facilitate a stronger learning link between school and home.

Despite the clear initial uptick in interest in the computers and regular usage in the months after their introduction, does this pattern persist over time? Anecdotal stories of problems with hardware that prevent usage, lack of sufficient facilities to charge laptops, and insufficient connection between the XOs and the formal curriculum of the school in many deployments would lead us to expect a decline in usage over time. The horror stories of closets full of unused XO computers that are shared by some critics of our project are, we judge, grossly exaggerated. That being said, providing the required infrastructure, appropriate service, and support for the hardware, as well as the right support for using the laptops for learning has been a key lesson for us over the past few years.

Type of Usage

As Robert Kozma, an international expert in educational technology at the non-profit research institute SRI, stated, "there is no consistent relationship between the mere availability or use of ICT and student learning."[9] It is vital to take a closer look at the *particular ways* in which students are engaging with their laptops.

Data from Plan Ceibal indicate that the introduction of the XO and Sugar software causes an interesting and important shift in the ways in which students use computers. Surveys of computer usage before and after deployment of the XOs show a marked change in behavior: prior to getting the XOs, children used computers almost exclusively for gaming. One year into the OLPC deployment, they were still using their computers to play games, but a substantial portion of their computer time was spent searching for information on the Internet, writing, drawing, chatting, making music and videos, sending e-mail, and blogging. Likewise, in a summer camp in Haiti that used XOs, student usage was tracked, showing that of the seventeen activities then available on the XO, four of these (Record, Write, Browse Internet, and Paint) represented 88 percent of laptop usage for camp participants. Cain Abel, an eleven-year-old boy who makes a living shining shoes in Arequipa, Peru, illustrates this same pattern of usage when he describes his time with his XO laptop:

> My laptop is my friend, like my sister. When I am home alone, I turn it on, and I can play. If I don't feel like playing, I write stories. What I like most is to draw. I also like the Wikipedia, because you can find everything there. It is like a gigantic library.

Critics dismiss some of these activities—such as chatting—as being among the less sophisticated and presumably less valuable uses of a computer; however, when the primary goals are literacy and creativity, engagement in an activity that directly encourages children to read and write or to engage their artistic selves is arguably a positive result.

In addition to showing a shift to different activities with the laptop, the available data support a differentiated pattern of use of the laptops for children of different ages. For example, the ACER report from the Solomon Islands indicated that younger students tended to use the laptop to learn to read, type words, and learn mathematics; older children used them to write stories, connect to the Internet, play games, and create videos. The older students also were more likely to engage in self-guided learning activities, using their XO as tools to explore and create, as well as to collaborate and learn with their fellow students. This, again, is in line with one of our emerging learnings, namely that providing a foundation of basic skills and knowledge accelerates student ability to use the laptops to build higher-order skills.

Impact on Student Learning

When assessing student learning, it is important to differentiate between acquisition of knowledge—the reading, writing, and arithmetic that are the stuff of traditional formal education—and capability building in those areas of most importance to proponents of constructionist learning theory—creativity, innovation, and authentic problem solving.

Current evaluation of the impact of the introduction of the XOs on knowledge acquisition is still preliminary, yet positive. Five months after the school in Arahuay, Peru, received XO laptops, teachers reported advances in reading comprehension, with fewer children failing and more performing at an advanced level; similar results were reported for math. Given OLPC's contention that learning happens in community, we looked outside the classroom, and there teachers reported increased communication between children in and out of class and increased sharing of ideas. The Associated Press, reporting on Arahuay, said: "Doubts about whether poor, rural children can benefit from quirky little computers evaporate as quickly as the morning dew in this hilltop

Andean village, where 50 primary school children got machines from the One Laptop per Child project six months ago."[10]

Data from the Doomadgee State School, a primary school in largely indigenous North West Queensland, Australia, indicate a 31 percent increase in understanding of numeric concepts numeracy for year three students—with the XO incorporated as a key component or engagement strategy. In a nearby school in Niue, in the South Pacific, after the first two years of the program, a clear increase in children's computer literacy and knowledge of global issues such as climate change was visible. A recent report from OLPC in Jamaica indicated a 12 percent increase in math scores after the XO was introduced into classrooms.[11] In mathematics, in particular, the XO and Sugar seem to help make learning fun; students are more motivated to learn math using Sugar activities than when they use a textbook. In the OLPC deployment in Ethiopia, since the content of the game-based activities was, in this case, nearly identical to the textbook, teachers could assign students a period of class time on the XO to support their learning.

That OLPC deployments also pay attention to factors such as social-emotional intelligence and cultivation of multiple sources of intelligence as vital measures of the success of the program would, a decade ago, have been highly controversial. Increasingly, however, the traditional education system is recognizing the importance of these factors as measures of student development. In a recent presentation, the OLPC Peru program team summed up this mindset shift well:

> Educational communities have come to understand that standardized tests are not the only dimension for measuring impact. Other factors such as the ability to solve problems, critical thinking and the use of multiple sources of information . . . and capability for self-directed learning are the new dimensions for measuring impact.[12]

The best means of assessing the acquisition of these types of skills by students is by taking a step back to gauge the nature of the activities in the classroom, including interaction between teacher and students and peer-to-peer interaction, as well as by observing student self-directed usage of the XOs. In other words, since constructionism focuses on "learning as doing," it is difficult to gauge the presence of vital skills by doing anything other than noticing whether students engage in constructionist activities.

An OLPC classroom tends to look chaotic in that the children do not sit in rows, silent, with all eyes forward. Rather, they work together, cluster around each other, and share their discoveries. In most schools in which the XO is introduced, we see a clear pattern of increase in group learning activities, collaboration, and idea sharing among students. We also see significantly more peer learning than in the traditional classroom. For example, data from Plan Ceibal in Uruguay show that 45 percent of children learn how to use the XO from peers. They also show that nearly 70 percent taught someone else to use the XO, including parents, siblings, other children and, in some cases, teachers.[13]

Although OLPC has been widely criticized as being anti-teacher, we have consistently recognized the importance of an adult "facilitator" of learning in supporting children in the adoption of the XOs for learning. The bulk of the misunderstanding likely stems from our insistence that the XO (and the underlying constructionist theory) enables a student-centered (as opposed to classroom- or school-centered) approach to learning, in which the specific curriculum is less important than the approach to learning. In an OLPC classroom, the teacher plays a vital role; he or she moves from group to group, prompting students with questions and encouraging them to push themselves to the next level. A principal in the Solomon Islands, for example, noted that the XO program made "classrooms come 'alive' by 'providing teachers with a dynamic, lively and resourceful learning aid.'"[14]

Stories of teachers facing difficulties making the transition from an instructionist to a constructionist approach to teaching populate most deployment evaluations. This inevitably leads to less classroom use of the laptop. For a teacher to make this transition generally requires some training *and* a leap of faith. Since the quality and quantity of training has varied so much from deployment to deployment, the pace of change has also varied. In Paraguay, where there is superlative support, the transition is rapid. In Peru, where most teachers are working in isolation, it has been slower. (Those programs that have utilized after-school and weekend "camps" have seen good progress; this informal setting, in which there is no pressure on the teachers to adhere to a set curriculum allows them to gain the experience and confidence needed to best utilize the laptop for learning.) Australia has taken perhaps the most rigorous and systemic approach to teacher training, with teachers attending an initial workshop, participating in an online continuing education program (for which they can earn certifications accredited by the Ministry of Education) and also participating in a social media site for teachers. In this way, teachers have an opportunity to watch each other learn and support one another's learning.

The teachers who fully embrace this different approach to learn-ing and see the results for their students tend to share their successes. Sdenka Zobeida Salas Pilco, a teacher from Puno (a small city in south-western Peru) wrote a 100-page book, *The XO Laptop in the Classroom*, which has become so popular among teachers that it has been trans-lated into five languages, including Arabic. Guzmán Trinidad, a physics teacher from Montevideo, has designed a number of science experi-ments that can be done for negligible cost using the laptop; when he is not in his own classroom, Trinidad gives workshops throughout the country about how to run these experiments. Rosamel Norma Ramírez Mendez, a teacher from central Uruguay is exceptional in her use of the laptop for learning and, fortunately for Uruguay, generous with her ac-complishments. Driven by a passion to share her experiences, successes, and failures with other teachers, she maintains an extensive blog, leads

THROWING THE STICK AWAY

In Abuja, Nigeria, a teacher who was accustomed to using a stout stick to maintain discipline with his unruly students noticed that after the introduc-tion of the XOs he could throw the stick used for corporal punishment out the window, as he observed that it wasn't needed: the children were en-thusiastically engaging in their work without the need of any "prompting."

discussions online (using e-mail and social media such as Facebook), and participates in national forums.

Impact on Teachers

Pulling back for a moment from the focus on constructionist learning by students to lessons for the introduction of laptops in the classroom, it is clear that the XOs must be "supported by teachers who know how to use the technology and can integrate it into their pedagogical practices."[15] As simple a statement as this is, it is a far cry from the current culture of use of technology by teachers in the developed world, let alone for developing countries where access to Internet and computers is not yet widespread.[16] In only a handful of Latin American countries—including Cuba, Chile, Costa Rica, and Uruguay—do more than 80 percent of teachers use computers regularly.[17] In general, this use is simply for looking up information rather than anything more sophisticated (only 50 percent of teachers in these countries had e-mail accounts as of 2011). Teacher-training programs also tend to pay minimal attention to technology; even in the United States until quite recently, teacher training regarding integration and use of technology has been limited at best.

OLPC has encountered significant resistance from teachers in many of our implementations. What is clear is that without engaging teachers in designing the deployment, providing sufficient technical training and support, as well as support in integrating the XO into the curriculum, the potential of the XOs for teaching more often than not remains unrealized. The IADB study of OLPC in Peru shows that the pattern until recently was to provide minimal teacher training; although in 89 percent of schools at least one teacher received training, only 10 percent of teachers reported receiving technical support and only 7 percent reported receiving support in integrating the XO into their curriculum. This is far below the level of support needed to support the bulk of teachers in their transition to a more facilitative approach to teaching.

Where teachers are supported, data assessing the impact of technology on teachers directly show that, like students, teachers are by and large motivated by the presence of the laptops. Many report that they receive practical benefits from the introduction of the XOs as well. Teachers surveyed in the IADB study in Peru reported that the laptops made it easier for them to plan for class and prepare materials, facilitated higher quality teaching, and supported the use of active learning strategies that engaged students more fully. Teachers indicated that they had less need to write on the blackboard in class, and that it both increased their ability to plan ahead for the week or term and made it easier overall to prepare lesson plans and provide homework to students. Teachers in the Solomon Islands noted that they could more easily record children's activities, monitor progress, and track assignments.

Importantly, introduction of the XO may increase the probability (and ease) of teachers' engaging in differentiated instruction that is better tailored to the individual needs of their students. In often crowded classrooms in developing country contexts, with students of different ages and markedly different skill levels, this could have significant impact. Teachers feel it may be more possible to customize lesson plans to meet the diverse needs of their students; they can provide supplemental materials to remedial learners and provide additional activities for their faster learners.

RIPPLE EFFECT ON FAMILIES AND COMMUNITIES

In its original conception, OLPC assumed that widespread impact on communities and societies would be driven by individual student learners who garnered new types of skills and had a sense of self-efficacy that would enable them to engage differently in their economies and societies. We also see ripple effects on parents and communities of introducing the XOs. For parents, the introduction of the XO induces a shift in their attitudes toward education for their children. As Brian Bird, the principal at Patukae in the Solomon Islands, explained, parents were both more engaged in and more supportive of education for their children. In Rwanda, teachers and administrators at OLPC schools indicated greater family involvement in the day-to-day education of children, with parents requesting the chance to learn how to use the laptops for themselves. In many cases, however, attitudes remain entrenched, as in Cambodia where Elaine Negroponte, cofounder of the original school in Reaksmy and head of Cambodia PRIDE, a small education non-profit, continues to fight the tendency of parents to remove students after, or sometimes during, primary school so that they can work to provide economic benefits to the family.

If one of the original goals of OLPC was to drive an equalization of access to information and learning in often highly stratified developing country societies, there is some emerging evidence of impact. In many cases, the receipt of the XO is the first experience these children will have of society showing a willingness to invest in them; it becomes an important indicator of their value. In Haiti, for example, there is a "general perception of the XO laptop as a symbol of opportunity and progress."[18] In Afghanistan, XOs have been distributed to both male *and female* students of primary-school age. The laptop, combined with the availability of Internet access and the mesh network, has enabled girls to be included in an educational system that has excluded them in the past. Attending school from home through the Internet has become an acceptable way for some to circumvent social taboos.

Uruguayan President Vázquez explicitly launched Plan Ceibal "to promote social justice by promoting equal access to information and communication tools for all our people."[19] From the outset, his goal was enhancing social equality. From the perspective of equality of access to technology, his policy was a success: as of the writing of this book, *every* child in Uruguay has a laptop computer and free Internet access. In fact, Uruguay is the only country in the world where the per-household penetration of computers is *inversely* proportional to household income (in part because the poor families tend to have more children). From the point of view of social inclusion in access to technology, Uruguay is unequivocally a success.

Most other deployments shared Vázquez's goal of universal access, but have not realized it to the extent of Plan Ceibal. Peru, for example, has fallen short in terms of numbers (there are more XOs in Peru than in Uruguay, but many more children) and connectivity (the challenge of providing Internet access anywhere but in coastal urban areas has been formidable). In the Solomon Islands, equality of access might have been feasible, but the sheer cost of Internet access has been prohibitive and has forced may schools to terminate their programs after only a few years.

There is more to the question of social inclusion than simply access. "Simply put, when children are just handed computers without any accompanying technical or social support, usage tends to be stratified."[20] Youth from low-income households presumably have fewer family members who are familiar with and use technology as well as guardians who work longer hours; they tend toward more basic uses of the computer such as chatting, playing games, or downloading media. In this case, again, the conversation comes full circle to the importance of an engaged and able adult as a facilitator of learning.

LIMITATIONS OF CURRENT EVIDENCE

In the 2009 Solomon Islands evaluation, participants were asked about the true objective of introducing the XOs into schools. Very different opinions emerged from those involved in the pilot. Some noted that the XOs are meant to "increase and equalize access to educational resources," while others note that they aim to "help children with poor or low levels of literacy" or provide a boost to "under-resourced schools." Some felt that the laptops were most helpful for improving teacher quality, while others focused on the simple objective of introducing children to technology. All of these are important pieces of OLPC's intent to use technology to drive a new type of student learning. However, the lack of clear and consistent understanding of the goal of the project (and hence the measures for gauging success) is notable and points to the complexity of the evaluation challenge for OLPC.

How should we define success? Is it economic development, education, or both? Do we measure it directly or indirectly? Comprehensive evaluation of OLPC's effectiveness requires a multivariate and multi-layered approach. We have been taking an active role in promoting an unconventional definition of "success" as well as an unconventional means of measuring it. We aim beyond traditional measures of educational outcomes, looking at "learning" and its applicability to social and economic development. We suscribe to a model of differentiated assessment, which makes learning visible to the student to foster reflection and self-direction, acknowledges and celebrates learning and communicates the learning to families and communities.

In addition to serving the needs of learning through assessment, OLPC also has to serve the needs of stakeholders—those who are investing tens and hundreds of millions of dollars in laptops, infrastructure, and training. We need to facilitate their strategic decision-making process and ensure that they have the data necessary to improve their deployments along the way and to evaluate the ultimate impact of their investment.

We can likely all agree that we need to be investing in education; to fail to do so is demonstrably "penny-wise and pound-foolish" as the social and economic cost of ignorance is too high.[21] The real question, however, is whether—given the range of potential educational investments—OLPC is the best investment to ensure a real transformation in the lives of children in the developing world. We are dissatisfied with the depth of our data and the strength of our conclusions. For now, our assessments of impact are inconclusive. With the objective of both informing teachers and learners and informing current and potential investors, available data are partial, at best, and do not draw a clear line of causation between the introduction of the XO and the learning outcomes cited, nor do they tell a clear, consistent, and well-supported story at this point about impact. What we might say with confidence is that the introduction of the XO is, at a minimum, a force for increasing engagement in school and for opening the door to increased motivation to learn. With this door open, evidence points to a clear and consistent impact of the XO in exposing children to a broader range of information about the world (harking back to Negroponte's original observation about children in Cambodia having knowledge of formerly unknown Brazilian soccer teams), enhancing knowledge and, importantly, enabling the type of self-guided learning and authentic problem solving that empowers students to be lifelong learners and, ultimately, agents of social change.

With a clear framework for monitoring and evaluation in place, and time to test the patterns over time in usage of the technology and impact on student learning outcomes, the next few years present the first real opportunity to put OLPC's theory of change fully to the test. At the same time that we are embarked on this next phase of our evolution in evaluation, we see increasingly positive signs of shift in the educational establishment in the direction of incorporating technology, as well as the tenets of constructionism, into the classroom. We also see strong anecdotal evidence of the impact of our program when thoughtfully deployed and thoroughly supported.

LESSONS AND REFLECTIONS

As Peru's champion for use of technology in learning, Oscar Becerra, explains, for better or for worse, amassing the necessary body of evidence of the impact (or lack thereof) of implementing technology to improve education will be "neither magic nor fast" and requires both commitment and persistence to be fully realized.

- *Manage measurement.* You *will* be evaluated and held accountable to stakeholders, so build measurement into what you do. Your metrics should consider outcomes—what happened—and process—how it happened. OLPC's measure of how many laptops were shipped to port of entry is an important outcome, but only for the first stage of our mission. Measurement must support evaluation of success, end to end for your project.
- *Defining the right metrics for success.* For those outside the social sector, running a non-profit social enterprise is often thought to be significantly simpler than running a for-profit organization, perhaps because the missions of most non-profits are so well-defined and they tend to be, by and large, smaller in

size. The reality, however, is that non-profit leaders are in two businesses at once: they have to ensure a clear and compelling model that drives desired impact for their target beneficiaries, and simultaneously ensure a compelling value proposition for potential funders. On the funding side, the metric for success is a diverse set of recurring funding streams. However, the ability to secure these funding streams depends in no small part on how the organization messages its mission and measures its impact.

- *Manage how you are measured.* Know how you will measure your success, or others will define it for you . . . with the likely outcome being criticism, perhaps uninformed and unwarranted. You will be held accountable for measurement, so make sure it is done right. Try to control the dialog about what it is you are aiming to impact, i.e., have a clear theory of change. OLPC has been criticized from the points of view of "computer assisted learning," "computer literacy," and "traditional learning." But our real focus is on creativity and problem-solving skills, which we have only recently begun measuring in a systemic way.

- *There is a troll under every bridge.* You will get criticized, so be prepared for it. Some criticism will be deserved and some unmerited. Some of the criticism will come from sources you may consider ignorant of what you are trying to accomplish, so you must constantly reinforce your message. In the case of OLPC, there has been an ongoing misunderstanding of our pedagogy: being child-centric is not the same as being anti-teacher. (Learning through doing is not the same as learning on your own.) When all eyes are on your project, every blemish will be on display. There will be criticism; you will need a thick skin, but not a thick skull—there is often a seed of wisdom in a critic's comments. Listen to the criticism, don't let it get you down, and learn from your mistakes and from your critics.

- *Have strong ideas, loosely held.* Test your assumptions and be prepared to evolve your model. Use data to identify your core drivers of impact. In our case, we opened up an important dialog about the ongoing centrality of the hardware to our desired impact for young learners in developing countries. Could we, in fact, get most of the way toward our goal just by focusing on the learning software? In assessing the "impact of OLPC," the evidence might be pointing instead toward "the impact of Sugar" in driving learning.

- *Be a learning organization.* The foundation of OLPC's new deployment approach is a structured and consistent approach to evaluation that enables our deployments to adjust in order to drive desired student, teacher, and community outcomes. Create a connected learning environment so your clients (deployments) can also learn. Specifically, enable data aggregation and sharing to promote learning across deployments.

PART 3

LOOKING AHEAD

EIGHT

OLPC NOW AND IN THE FUTURE

"Who dares to teach must never cease to learn."

—John Cotton Dana

"OLPC will . . . should it succeed, serve as a new model for getting the nonprofit, private, and public sectors to work together efficiently and productively. . . . There are problems too big to be solved by NGOs or corporations (or governments, for that matter)—problems that demand new kinds of alliances. OLPC is, in that sense, not just building a new computing machine. It's also building a new philanthropic machine, one as cobbled together and untraditional as the $100 laptop. The question that remains is just how well either of those machines will really work."

—James Surowiecki, *Technology Review*, November 2006

IN 2010, AHMAD ASHKAR, A FIRST-YEAR GRADUATE STUDENT AT the Cambridge, Massachusetts, campus of the Hult International Business School—a for-profit business school (and incidentally the fastest-growing business school in the world)—attended a lecture about OLPC given by Charles Kane in his social entrepreneurship class. While listening to the challenges the organization was facing, Ashkar had an idea: why not hold a contest to elicit ideas for how to enable a step-function change in the impact that OLPC was driving? Having grown up as a Palestinian refugee living in Gaza, Ashkar had a personal interest in improving education in environments like this and was curious about how to expand OLPC in his home country. His initial idea was to leverage Hult's five global campuses—located in Boston, San Francisco, London, Dubai, and Shanghai—to host teams from business schools around the world in a competition. The teams would react to a case study of OLPC and present ideas for how to improve the organization and/or innovate on the program model. One team would be chosen from each of the five global campuses, and the five winners would compete for a global case challenge title.

Case challenges and business-plan competitions have a long history in business schools of marshaling the talent of students to solve real-world problems by engaging them in project-based/solution-based learning; Ashkar's innovation is to apply these traditional business tools to the social-impact causes. Fast forward three years: Hult is now sponsoring the Hult Global Case Challenge, which it bills as "the world's largest crowd-sourcing initiative dedicated to solving global social challenges." In 2012, the Hult Challenge brought together MBA students from more than one hundred business schools from all over the world and tasked them with solving the strategic and operational challenges of reaching global scale.

In 2012, three social-impact organizations were the focus of the competition: in the education sector, OLPC; in housing, Habitat for Humanity; and in energy, SolarAid (an organization dedicated to eliminating kerosene stoves, one of the leading causes of child deaths in Africa). Former President Bill Clinton was a keynote speaker and judge in the 2011 contest; in 2012 the Clinton Global Initiative co-sponsored the initiative, with Clinton again serving as a judge, joined by Muhammad Yunus, founder of the Grameen Bank. Student teams developed proposals that identified the key barriers to global impact for these three organizations and proposed solutions. Ultimately, winning teams for each organization presented in a final head-to-head, and the organization whose team won the competition received US$1 million to implement the proposal.

Hundreds of teams from eighty-four schools participated in the education track. In the first year of the contest, the winning team was from the Tepper Graduate Business School at Carnegie Mellon University. They proposed to create an "app store" for educational software and services that would enhance Sugar appliances and involve more entrepreneurial participation from the global software-development community. In 2012, the team from the American University of Iraq proposed that IT students in their final semester of school, as part of their degree, provide computer training to marginalized women. These women will teach children and teachers in secondary schools how to use the computers, and they will be responsible for distributing the computers to the children. The team from Hult's San Francisco campus proposed a social-impact bond as a way to finance not only the purchase of laptops, but also funding support for infrastructure and training.

The ideas for OLPC that have emerged from the Hult Challenge fall into two broad categories. The majority of ideas focus on identifying a barrier or gap to the efficiency or effectiveness of a specific aspect of OLPC's theory of change and propose a solution (such as the "app store"). Some ideas, however, start with a premise that even the most fundamental elements of OLPC's approach are open for reinvention. The team from the Columbia University School of Social Work focused not on the XO, but rather on Sugar and the importance of enabling broad distribution of the learning tools as a the key to driving impact. In a more radical step, one team recommended that OLPC abandon both hardware sales and Sugar and instead focus on developing learning software for Android devices. Ideas of this type are always harder for us to hear as they force us to question our most basic assumptions. At the same time, they are critically important because they force that deep self-assessment.

These two categories of ideas, evolutionary and revolutionary, are both critical to the sustainability and growth of OLPC and any social organization. The challenge we face—and the challenge we invite you to help us to address—is how to balance the forces of evolutionary and revolutionary growth. How do we serve and support our current users while expanding to reach a broader audience?

EVOLVING OLPC

Ptolemy I asked Euclid, his math tutor, if there was an easier way to study geometry. Euclid replied, "Sire, there is no royal road to geometry." Some problems are inherently hard and there is no shortcut or easy path to success; that has certainly been our experience over the past decade. Since its founding, OLPC has worked hard to continually improve upon the four critical areas of our operations: hardware, software, enabling sales, and our approach to deployment. As you read previously, we have also evolved significantly in terms of our operational structure (with the split into the Association, the Foundation, and Sugar Labs), exploring different approaches for how best to organize ourselves to achieve our mission most efficiently. All the examples that follow represent important evolutionary, or incremental, improvements to OLPC's activities based on both our own "learning from doing" and the advice and analysis of countless individuals and organizations who have partnered with us or simply studied our approach and impact.

Hardware: The Evolving XO Laptop

OLPC has made significant improvements to the XO hardware over time: while the exterior of the machine retains the form and coloring of the original XO (the "green machine"), internally it is a wholly different machine. The introduction of the ARM-based XO 1.75 in 2012 enabled OLPC to finally (more than seven years after the idea was conceived) reach its goal of providing an ultra–low-power (less than two watts) laptop that would meet the requirements of human or inexpensive solar power. This, along with other enhancements such as a touch screen, has enabled us to come close to realizing the machine we had envisioned in 2005. The XO has also needed to evolve both to remain on the cutting edge of balancing performance, cost, and power; and to be able to compete relative to the expanding range of options now open to volume buyers. (The global netbook market appears to have peaked in late 2009 and is in part being supplanted by low-cost tablets and smartphones.)

Tablets appear to represent a significant shift in how people use computers—at least for content consumption, such as browsing, reading, and viewing. In keeping with the shift toward tablet-like devices such as the iPad, OLPC introduced a next-generation XO tablet, loaded with touch-enabled Sugar software, at the 2012 Consumer Electronics Show. It was well received by reviewers, lauded in particular for its attention to low power consumption, as well as the fact that the ARM processor would allow it to be powered by a small, inexpensive solar panel. These innovations open up a number of new possibilities for simplifying deployment in environments lacking consistent power. Note that neither the tablet nor the touch-only version of Sugar software are fully product-ready at the time this book is being written.

The more significant change to computing in the past few years has been the growth in the smartphone market. Broadband connectivity is still not universal, but where it is available, it is becoming the low-cost, ubiquitous platform for Internet access, e-mail, and text messaging (e.g., SMS). Commensurate with the exponential growth of broadband and the smartphone has been a decline in the desktop and laptop market. For many consumers, these devices satisfy their computing needs. Broadband connectivity has not yet reached rural communities in the developing world, and therefore, moving in this direction to enable impact has not been on our radar screen. Nonetheless, access to voice and data communications has proved invaluable to OLPC. We are experimenting with using low-bandwidth phones to create a learning community for teachers. In rural Peru—and many other places where OLPC works—most teachers do not have Internet access, so e-mail communication and web-based social networking communities for teacher support are not available. However, most teachers do have access to mobile phones. We are currently exploring the possibility of creating a text-message support system for teachers in Peru where users can text questions and receive answers. They would also be able to access a limited-support network by the dynamic rerouting of traveling mentors to where they are needed most.

Software: Growing the Sugar Learning Environment

Since emerging from the early work of OLPC, the Sugar learning environment has innovated in two broad areas: spinning off into a separate organization through the creation of Sugar Labs and the continued development of the platform. When founding Sugar Labs in 2008, Bender had a clear vision for a zero-overhead, community-driven platform to extend and improve Sugar. By breaking Sugar away from OLPC, the community was freed up from the organizational constraints of OLPC and also—and more importantly—from the notion that Sugar is just for the XO.

Since it was spun out from OLPC, Sugar has evolved along three dimensions. The most obvious change has been one of scale. In early 2008, there were only tens of Sugar activities and only a handful of Sugar developers. Today, there are hundreds of activities and an equal number of developers. (The transition is not just due to the influx of professional programmers; an ever-increasing number of activities are being developed by Sugar users, including pre-teenage children.) A less visible change is the increased emphasis on providing learners and stakeholders with tools for self-assessment and program assessment. The portfolio tools have matured and the Sugar user interface has undergone extensive reengineering to better support the capture of data relevant to assessment. A third change—only visible to our developer community—is an increased engagement with the global Sugar community. As Sugar has matured, and the tool-chain upon which it is built continues to improve, it has become easier to leverage the work of the broader free software community. This has enabled us to incorporate new features, such as multi-touch support and accessibility tools, without having to divert our efforts away from our learning goals. It also means that Sugar will be more easily maintained.

At the 2010 LibrePlanet conference, Eben Moglen, founder of the Software Freedom Law Center, gave a talk about how much has been accomplished by the free-software community. He stated, boldly, that free software is no longer an option; it is "indispensable" to doing anything innovative at scale. OLPC, through its close association with

Sugar Labs, has been instrumental in raising awareness throughout the free-software ecosystem of the needs of the education community and in raising awareness within the education community of the power and cost-effectiveness of free software. While we wrestle daily at Sugar Labs with technical challenges, our primary challenge remains one of impressing upon the education community that a culture of collaboration and criticism is essential to learning.

Deployments: Getting Better at Getting XOs into the Hands of Children

Under the leadership of Rodrigo Arboleda and Robert Hacker, the OLPC Association has manufactured and distributed more than 2.5 million laptops. But the association does much more than sell laptops: it has been instrumental in helping deployments use these laptops effectively. In partnership with in-country clients, we help with all aspects of deployments, including logistics, security, maintenance and repair, system software, curriculum development, teacher training, and assessment.

In recent years, the OLPC Association has matured as an enterprise. Arboleda and Hacker together bring more than sixty years of experience in running successful multinational enterprises, so it is no surprise that they run a tighter, more focused operation than did the original set of academics from MIT. Perhaps more surprising is the creativity they bring to the enterprise. Currently the association is exploring local manufacturing partnerships, including the assembly of XOs in Rwanda. They also continue to develop public-private partnerships as a means to generate demand and to ensure that deployments are well managed. Finally, we continue to push innovative business models as a means to amass the capital necessary to launch large-scale initiatives.

Sales and Financing: Helping Clients Invest in Education

Lack of funding has delayed or eliminated adoption of OLPC in many countries. Countries simply do not have access to the large amount of money required to launch a program (recall that at the $188 price, the original, mandatory one-million-unit XO order requires an initial capital outlay of $188 million—a huge sum in countries where the average education expenditure per pupil per year is often less than US$1,000). Access to capital is the engine of capitalism. Where there is lack of access to capital, there is stagnation. There are limited numbers of sovereign bonds that are used to build roads or power plants, but amazingly, there are no bonds earmarked to address the challenge of improving education. This potential is causing great financial institutions of the world to turn their "financial engineering" prowess on this issue and leverage the arbitrage at hand. Education is a logical starting point for which to make thoughtful investments with low-risk returns.

At OLPC, we have been working on developing and testing a suite of financial tools that give government access to low-cost, long-term capital to finance education investments. One example is an "education bond" that would raise funds exclusively for the use of educational

EDUCATION BOND

Sovereign bonds are common in developing countries; they allow access to the world capital markets to secure funding for projects such as building roads or other economic enhancement projects. An education bond teams socially responsible investors in the capital markets to secure funding for educational initiatives such as building schools, electrifying, or Internet enabling a community and as important, providing computers to allow children to take full advantage of these educational initiatives. At the time of this writing, interest rates are at historical low levels, which makes even "junk-bond (high-risk) funding" within reach. Socially responsible investors can get a "market" return on their investment and have the security of investing for a good purpose. Nations can jump-start educational programs and pay back their borrowings over an extended time frame, such that their investment in an educated workforce can help pay for the original loans.

initiatives and make it easier for governments to choose to invest more of their capital in education. Education bonds are not simply about financing XO laptops. Funds can be used for a range of education-oriented infrastructure such as building schools, providing electricity, computers, and Internet access; and, on the services side, investing in improved teacher training and curriculum. All these factors can raise the level of learning in the developing world exponentially.

EVOLUTION VERSUS REVOLUTION

OLPC, like any organization, struggles with the tension between evolutionary and revolutionary growth. While the origins of OLPC are absolutely revolutionary, building and sustaining a global community of OLPC supporters and users has a natural predilection for the evolutionary track. The examples of recent innovations at the OLPC Association clearly show an evolutionary path. But we aspire to do much more than simply survive; as an organization, a community, and a movement for universal access to learning, we need to find the appropriate balance between incremental progress and radical reinvention.

Original Mission and Theory of Change

To consider the challenge of evolution versus revolution, it is helpful to revisit the original mission and then consider the changing context in which we have operated over the past seven years. From the beginning, the mission of OLPC has been to create opportunities for learning by all children in developing countries. Given the scope of our mission, it is not really unexpected that our goal has not been fully realized—with more than one billion school-age children growing up in developing countries, even millions of children "served" is minimal compared to the vast size of the overall problem. We can either celebrate the fact that we have directly impacted more than 2.5 million children, or we can lament the hundreds of millions of children we have yet to reach. Depending on the perspective you take, evolutionary or revolutionary change appears the right path. There is no single voice at OLPC to declare victory or determine next steps—but there is general consensus on two points. First, the impact we are looking to enable through getting XOs in the hands of children hasn't been consistent—the context in which each child is situated impacts the benefit derived from the XO. Second, we agree that the scale of impact is not big enough—while we celebrate the fact that we might have helped to turn the light on in the head of even a single child, our vision of impact remains broader.

OLPC's theory of change was built on filling three gaps in the educational system in most developing countries (and, we would argue, in developed countries as well). First, children lack access to the tools and information they need to unlock their learning potential. Second, although technology can fill this gap and give children access to the world of information, there was a lack of appropriate hardware (low-cost, low-power, ruggedized, and portable). Finally, there was an additional market gap in availability of an appropriate software program that was targeted at younger children and encouraged the type of learning that constructionism encouraged (i.e., authentic problem solving and room for innovation and creativity). While our theory of change hasn't altered, the world around us has shifted in significant ways in the past seven years: approaches to technology have changed, modes of access have changed, and perspectives on how children learn and are taught have changed. Each theme is critical to OLPC; what excites us is that all these changes feel like movement in the right direction.

In the world of education, we are seeing greater embrace of Piaget's constructivist and Papert's constructionist principles in education. More students, educators, and citizens are embracing the core idea that learning is the active process of making meaning and context at the intersection of experience and ideas. More people believe that education is about facilitating the discovery of meaning rather than imparting facts. In other words, the sage on the stage, it seems, is in the process of being retired.

It is no surprise that computer hardware has evolved substantially since the first XO laptop was built. We pioneered low-cost, low-power laptops, but today there are many manufacturers serving this market niche. The government of India has in successive years announced a $10 laptop, a $35 laptop, and, most recently, a $60 tablet computer.

A SOCIAL NETWORK FOR LEARNING

Fifteen years ago, Papert predicted that a social network among children would be a significant breakthrough in education. He referred to the example of Michele Evard, working at the James W. Hennigan Elementary School in Boston, who, in the mid-1990s, had created an online system to allow a student to throw a problem out to a virtual community of other students (and possibly teachers) to request solutions. Today, in our face-booked world, a social network is old news. But for children and teachers in developing countries, it is a revolution in the making. In Uruguay, the ability to connect teachers into a virtual learning community has supported their adoption of the XO and changed their approach to teaching through technology. And for students, one of the ideas to emerge from a recent competition for ways to drive innovation with the XO was the creation of an XO Network to connect kids around the world directly to one another.

While they have yet to deliver on *any* of these promises—even when including steep discounts through government subsidies—it is inevitable that they will eventually produce a reasonable product at a low enough price as to be appropriate for the education market in the subcontinent. Although we continue to believe that the XO platform is still in a class of its own in terms of quality and functionality—as of fall 2012, no one has come close to our energy efficiency or the quality of our display—nonetheless, the market will eventually catch up with us.

The software front has seen substantially less innovative competition, although the fundamental debate still rages as to whether or not a computer equipped with a traditional operating system and software designed for task-based work and content consumption is a viable option for education. One great improvement in the software space has been increased adoption of free software by governments and large corporations around the world. While the push-back regarding free software has lessened, there is significant pressure regarding two recent developments: cloud computing and Android. Both represent current areas of growth in the industry and each has certain advantages (and disadvantages) over Sugar's desktop model. We are debating how best to leverage these trends without sacrificing those attributes that are at the core of Sugar: collaboration, reflection, universal access, and the ability for anyone to appropriate and modify the code.

Finally, in the world of social development, we have seen a massive shift in how the developed world views the least developed countries—and recognizes the interdependence among all of us. Much attention, research, and debate has focused on the "bottom of the pyramid" (the more than 2.5 billion people in the world living on less than $2.50 per day). While the debate rages on between those who view the bottom of the pyramid as potential consumers, those who view them as entrepreneurs and innovators, and those who view them as business partners, the impact on OLPC is that more people, from more diverse backgrounds and interests, are paying attention to the children we intend to serve.

A BLANK SHEET OF PAPER

Let's imagine a complete reinvention of OLPC. We have so much more at our disposal than we had at the time we started: things we have built, things we have learned, momentum toward our vision, and some important changes in the surrounding context (in technology and education) that are moving in what we consider to be the right direction. While we have some ideas of how to go forward, we also know there are other, better ideas that have not yet emerged for us. We need ideas and assistance to reach scale. We present here three challenges that we are struggling with, and we invite you to help us solve them.

It Is Not Either/Or

When we launched OLPC, the working model was that we would solve for the toughest problem first and then everything else would fall into place. In our minds, the toughest problem was helping a single child, alone, under a tree, to learn how to learn. We would fix this worst case and work backward from there. We learned that perhaps the worst case is not the solitary student, but rather the student in the formal structure of the traditional classroom. Our approach has focused on children having informal time with the computers, but getting machines deployed at scale meant government buyers and classroom environments. And so was born a tension between classroom time and informal time.

The OLPC community, especially the network of in-country partners, has invested significant effort to integrate the XO and Sugar into the classroom curriculum, and we want to continue to leverage and expand that effort. Simultaneously, we continue to know that the most effective way children learn using computers is through informal time, and we are equally invested in understanding and scaling the learning and best practices for what it takes for children to engage in learning communities outside the classroom. Using as many shared resources as possible, we need to solve for these two scenarios (classroom and informal learning community) as well as any number of other solutions that others propose or that emerge from our work.

Requirements for Success

Regardless of whether our distribution model involves schools or after-school programs or something else, we have learned a lot about what is required for learning to take root and thrive. We need to build active and sustainable learning communities under widely differing conditions: different levels of income; different levels of communication; different levels of community trust; and different levels of valuing learning and children. Claudia Urrea's work to develop a global network of learners and Gómez Monroy's work to develop local learning communities as the basis for enabling real and sustainable learning are the harbingers of the future of OLPC. We believe that computers and the Sugar learning environment solve one of two binding constraints on universal access to learning—the second binding constraint is developing sustainable local learning communities. Learning communities are the key to both the breadth and depth of impact of the XO and Sugar.

Where Are We Unique, Best of Breed, or Lagging Behind?

The original vision for OLPC was that we would do only the work that we were uniquely qualified to do—we would leverage our talents and relationships to design an innovative laptop and learning environment

THE NEED FOR A "THIRD PLACE"

Ray Oldenburg argues in *The Great Good Place* that "third places"—community places between home and work (or school)—are important for civil society and civic engagement. At OLPC, we have also argued for the need of a third place where children can engage in informal learning. Whether at the Saturday learning clubs in Caacupé or vacation camps at the Holmes Elementary School in Miami, we have found that a third place provides the space necessary for learning in a supportive environment. Finding a third place in each OLPC deployment is the secret to success.

that would both serve the needs of children and be so economically attractive that the market would adopt the laptop and force it to become as inexpensive and ubiquitous as pencil and paper. Because we are driven and well connected to other driven people, we thought that we could attract others to come help us with continued innovation—not just on the laptop and software, but on all the challenges we knew we would eventually encounter—like deployments, curriculum integration, creating learning communities, and so forth.

As you know by this point in the book, things change. We have become an organization that at its heart still sits in a position to utilize the power of knowledge, academia, and big dreams to prove that a better future is possible. But we are also invested much more heavily in actually making that future a reality—and in doing so, we have taken on roles we did not plan for. In some of those roles we are unique, in some we are the best, and in some we have fallen behind the ability of others. In developing a strategy for universal impact, we need to leverage the increased focus on serving the least developed countries and the increased alignment with our educational beliefs to create broader partnerships that allow us to focus on our unique skills and adopt the best practices of others. For example, no matter how much we love the XO laptop, our edge in hardware is lessening over time. The XO3.0 tablet offers an interim solution. Another tactic is to revisit forming partnerships with other hardware makers in order to deploy Sugar more broadly. Still another approach could be to explore a partnership with a global network of Internet cafés, and in the process, create a sustainable local business that gives more children affordable access to Sugar. If any effort can provide a learning opportunity for more children, then we are interested in supporting its success.

BARRIERS OR CONVERGENCE?

There are three barriers that we believe must be simultaneously over-come for OLPC to have sustainable impact at scale: the tool divide, the learning divide, and the digital divide. The tool divide refers not just to the laptop, but to all the tools—hardware and software—required for both a teacher to teach and a child to learn. The learning divide refers to the intangible tools of learning and education: the pedagogy, training, and curriculum of learning that encompasses examples, problems, and lessons for both learners and educators to draw from—those things that facilitate the use of the laptop for learning. The digital divide refers to the ability of a person to access information and to communicate over distance—both critical resources for learning, collaboration, and support. In the OLPC context, the challenge of the digital divide is that it is fundamentally about infrastructure—power and communications, both of which have historically been expensive to build, maintain, and use and have therefore been built solely in support of the commerce that can afford to pay, with only minimal regard to enabling the social impact that the infrastructure has the power to unlock.

From its earliest point—while OLPC was still just an idea—we understood that each of these barriers was a binding constraint to sustainable and universal improvement in education and that we would need to address all of them simultaneously. And yet we are still known for the $100 laptop—a title that focuses us squarely and solely on solving the tool-divide problem.

While we believe that the key to success is found at the intersection of all three domains, there are examples of partial success that occur at the overlap of only two domains. The Khan Academy delivers more than 132 million lessons online to students wishing to explore "a library of over 3,000 videos covering everything from arithmetic to physics, finance, and history and 315 practice exercises," that allow students "to learn what you want, when you want, at your own pace."[1] Khan is offering a curriculum for self-directed learning. It is a useful resource, but not, we think, sufficient to teach children to learn.

In a story about his experiences teaching graduate-level physics in Brazil, Nobel laureate Richard Feynman provides some insight into the limitations of the Khan Academy approach. At the end of the academic year, Feynman gave a speech in which he demonstrated that no science was actually taught in Brazil because students only memorized what they heard or read—they didn't experiment, and therefore they did not truly know science. Feynman randomly selected a page from the national physics textbook and read the definition of triboluminescence: the light admitted when crystals are crushed.

> I said "And there, have you got science? No! You have only told what a word means in terms of other words. You haven't told anything about nature— what crystals produce light when you crush them, *why* they produce light. Did you ever see any student go home and *try* it? He can't.
>
> But if instead, you were to write, 'When you take a lump of sugar and crush it with a pair of pliers in the dark, you can see a bluish flash. Some other crystals can do that too. Nobody knows why. The phenomenon is called 'triboluminescence.' Then someone will go home and try it."[2]

Khan Academy represents a great resource, but it alone does not address the three barriers—it assumes Internet access and ignores integration of ideas into a learning context. Considered alone, Khan Academy is not sufficient.

At the intersection of the tools and learning domains are places like the Waldorf schools, which follow a pedagogy that embraces the development of the whole child through experiential hands on learning. The self-discovery aspects of the Waldorf approach share commonalities with constructionism, but differ in that the Waldorf program eschews technology. Those who endorse this approach say computers inhibit creative thinking, movement, human interaction, and attention spans.[3]

The Waldorf model is highly regarded and effective, but it seems impossible to scale to anything approaching global impact. We also disagree with the negative view of computers: they offer the potential for a nearly limitless learning environment, scale, and customization to the needs and interests of individual children.

Examples of the overlap of learning tools and the digital divide are found in the efforts to create online teacher development and mentoring programs. The New Teacher Center's eMSS (e-Mentoring for Student Success) platform is a content-specific online mentoring program that supports professional growth and development and increases the retention of science, technology, engineering, and math (STEM) and special education teachers in the United States.[4] Often, STEM and special education teachers are spread thin in school systems and have little time or opportunity to receive or provide subject matter-specific training and development support. eMSS creates an online community for these widely distributed teachers to share ideas and learn from one another effectively. The New Teacher Center program offers an invaluable resource for teachers to develop effective communities of practice that are geographically dispersed, and it represents a class of critical solutions necessary to support the growth and development of teaching skills that enhance teacher effectiveness.

The future of OLPC starts with restating and re-embracing our original ideals and re-centering ourselves at the nexus of the three divides. The future of OLPC may well be solution agnostic: we have already unbundled our IP and process knowledge of hardware, software, and deployments in order to embrace any solution that achieves measurable and sustainable impact—at any scale. And we are embracing two ideas that our clients and fellow practitioners are promoting: (1) all progress toward our ultimate goal is good, if not necessarily fair; and (2) there is not likely to be one best solution. In order to deliver at scale sustainable technology to enable children to "learn to learn"—to form a mutually reinforcing system for learning, sharing, and teaching—we must find solutions to the tool divide, the learning divide, and the digital divide. Children and teachers need tools (most likely computers) that enable solution-based learning; they need a curriculum, environment, and community of supportive educators; and both students and teachers need access to the rich content and communication over distance that the Internet provides.

LESSONS AND REFLECTIONS

In chapter 1 of this book, we posed some questions facing social enterprises. Throughout the book, we have touched on partial answers to these questions in the context of OLPC. We close here with some final lessons and reflections that are shaping OLPC now and in the future:

- *Build the organization that can do the job.* Get great at something: have a great idea and then get great at executing it. OLPC did have a great idea and assembled a great engineering team to execute (part of) it. Over time, we assembled a great business team as well, which has brought us closer to our goal. And we're now learning what it takes to support excellence in deployment and, importantly, what OLPC (with our necessarily limited human and other resources) can reasonably do to support this.
- *Innovators have to lead.* Entrepreneurship implies some degree of innovation. If you want to remain on the cutting edge, you must create a space for innovation inside your organization, and dedicate people, time, and resources to thinking differently. Remember that the people who want to lead the revolution do not want to run the office. Either house innovation intelligently or park it outside of your organization. OLPC adopted the latter model when it bifurcated into a foundation (innovation) and association (operation), although to the outside observer, it is still just one organization.
- *Creative destruction is sometimes necessary for growth.* Your sense of what must be done—your theory of action—will change over time, and you need to be willing and able to evolve your organization along with it. Cannibalizing an existing organization (or market) in order to make room for new

products and services is one of the more difficult tasks for any
enterprise, and social enterprises must occasionally rise to this
challenge as well. That said, innovators should create and then
defer to management as to how to leverage their innovations, or
they may inadvertently destroy the very organization they are
trying to build. Case in point, the public "promise" of a tablet
from OLPC has resulted in potential customers deferring their
decision to deploy OLPC.

- *Getting creative about financing is going to be increasingly
  important to enabling scale.* Quite simply, growth requires
  access to capital. How your project is financed is *the* key
  question you must answer in order to grow a product-based
  social enterprise. At OLPC, we have been on the cutting edge
  of thinking about how to address some of the constraints that
  our non-profit structure has placed on us regarding access to
  traditional funding sources. Although some of these efforts
  have not yet borne fruit, we have been thinking creatively
  about how to leverage traditional financial instruments
  as well as considering the costs and benefits of alternative
  organizational forms.

NINE

A CALL TO ACTION

"Our goal is to create a generation of critical thinkers with the capability to solve problems, establishing a culture of thinking and of independent learning."

—Walter Bender

"Innovation is at its most powerful when it works through imagination. While creative solutions are important, the power of imagination takes innovation to a new level, because when we create with imagination, we are not simply responding to a problem; we are building worlds."

—John Seely Brown, former director of
the legendary Xerox PARC

WHEN WE SET OUT TO WRITE THIS BOOK, WE HAD three goals. One goal was to tell the real story of One Laptop per Child. We strove to separate the hype about a very high profile, global initiative from the concrete accomplishments of the organization and of the individuals who have contributed (in many cases donated) their time, energies, and creativity in service of a mission in which they strongly believed. We also aimed to shed light on some of our successes: We were one of the first organizations to engage in product-driven and distributed, network-based social change. We were early pioneers in laptop technology and learning software for children, and we were among the first to envision the possibility of fully revolutionizing a broken educational system, as well as to believe in the possibility of this revolution taking place in the most challenging developing country environments.

A second goal was equally as important: to give others a chance to learn from our success and, just as much, from our mistakes. We really do believe that you can learn from the examples of others in a way that will accelerate your own success. We walked down a path without really knowing where we were going. And we made many mistakes—big and small—along the way. But by laying bare the various steps we took along our path and by bringing attention to lessons learned along the way, we hope to have acquainted you with some of the basic issues you might confront should you choose to leave the books behind and take action to drive social change. We have tried to tell you not just who did what, but also how and why. We tried to be clear about both the challenges we encountered and the mistakes we made, as well as the lessons we learned from them. We hope that the people who come after us will benefit from a clearer perspective on what we did and did not do, and the results that these choices drove.

Our third goal was to inspire you, potentially in a couple of ways. We hope that our passion for the mission was evident in our writing and that it inspires some of you to take action in a manner similar to that of Cecilia Rodriguez Alcalá from Paraguay Educa or Oscar Becerra in Peru—entrepreneurs who are advancing our mutual social cause. We would like nothing more than for readers to engage with the OLPC Association and Sugar Labs to support our mission of educating every child in the world. We are equally excited about the possibility of motivating even one person to challenge himself or herself to see new possibilities and take on the challenges of social innovation and social entrepreneurship to address an issue that is blocking our world—and the people in it—from achieving their full potential. Sadly, the world does not lack for endemic social problems begging for solutions. Take up the challenge of the one that touches you and answer the call to action.

LESSONS FROM *LEARNING TO CHANGE THE WORLD*

The title of this book, *Learning to Change the World,* was chosen to reflect two critical meanings. First, that learning is the key to creating a better world. In 1897 John Dewey wrote, "Education is a regulation of the process of coming to share in the social consciousness." In other words, the extent to which we educate our children will strongly influence the extent to which the world in which we live evolves in positive new directions or, conversely, the extent to which it devolves and disintegrates. Learning—true learning that broadens the mind and enables the visualization and realization of new possibilities—is fundamental for empowerment at the unit of one—at the level of an individual. And, it is the basic DNA of better societies, better economies, and more broadly enjoyed human prosperity.

The title also reflects the fact that OLPC aims to be, at our core, a true learning organization. For all that we have deeply and strongly held beliefs about technology and education, our real focus since the project began has been learning about what works both in education reform and in driving social change. We have structured our macro-level learning into three sections: themes from our experience in education and learning; themes from our experiences as social innovators and social entrepreneurs; and finally, themes from our experience as part of a social-change movement that extends far beyond OLPC. What we have learned is based on experiences specific to our program, but we hope and expect that at least some of our lessons will be applicable to a wider audience of agents of social change—both current and future.

Learning about Education

We have learned that the laws of mass and inertia apply to social causes just as they apply to the physical world: a body in motion tends to stay in motion, and a body at rest tends to stay at rest. We went in knowing that education changes at a glacial pace—that it is a massive global enterprise that lumbers along, mostly in the direction it is already heading. Papert's story of Victorian-era school teachers time-traveling to modern times hammers home the point that our fundamental approach to how we educate our children has not changed in hundreds of years. Nearly fifty years after constructionist ideas were articulated and introduced, and more than a century after John Dewey began expounding his views on education, we are only now seeing real signs that these concepts are being embraced by the education establishment. And that evolution of education theory is by no means evenly distributed around the world. The vast majority of developing economies continue to embrace and enforce the pedagogy of rote memorization.

The development and use of technology for education is moving at a similarly slow pace. Despite nearly universal use of personal computers and the Internet in business settings, we see very little real integration of computers into the classroom. A 1971 survey by AIR (American Institute for Research) reported that, remarkably, 13 percent of US high schools had computers for instruction.[1] And yet, forty years later, George Kembel's description of the classroom where "[i]nstead of parking themselves in a lecture hall for hours, students will work in collaborative spaces, where future doctors, lawyers, business leaders, engineers, journalists and artists learn to integrate their different approaches to problem solving and innovate together" remains a vision for the future (2020), rather than a reality of today (2010).[2]

Even with the decades of very slow change, we continue to believe that we are at a point in history when revolutionary changes in learning and education are possible. Just as glaciers regularly calve off icebergs, abrupt changes occasionally occur. As we write this book, a chunk of ice fifteen times the size of Manhattan is breaking away from the Pine Island ice shelf in Antarctica—containing enough fresh water to meet the water needs of the United States for more than four years. As big as that sounds, it is only a tiny fraction of the ice shelf, and an insignificant percentage of polar ice caps. OLPC's 2.5 million computers in the hands of children are a similar story. If you buy into any aspect of our theory of change, a significant number of children have been helped; but it is just a drop in the bucket. OLPC alone is not going to scale its impact by three orders of magnitude; we need hundreds of efforts of equal or greater size to reach a billion children—and we need to be co-ordinating and learning from one another as we scale.

The need for coordination among efforts leads us directly to our second point: there are no silver bullets in the global problem of education. When we began to write this book, our working title was *It's Not (Just) about the Laptop*. Partly this was intended as a constant reminder to the authors as we worked that OLPC was always aiming to do much more than create a $100 laptop: we were intending to create an integrated solution of hardware, learning software, training, curriculum integration, and field support that could revolutionize education for young children in developing countries. But even those components of OLPC do not constitute a total answer. As we saw in researching the case studies, every deployment presented a unique environment, and succeeding in the variety of country contexts in which we have worked made it difficult (if not impossible) to create a standardized solution. The best we could achieve was constantly improving our core building blocks and attempting to flexibly deploy and adapt them to each new location.

"I Don't Know, but Neither Do You."

We are very proud of the XO and Sugar, and we continue to believe that the hardware and software are as good as, if not better than, other options available . . . in most cases. But, *most* cases does not mean *all* cases. The future of universal education reform requires us to embrace the complicated reality that we are attempting to solve multidimensional problems that manifest differently from place to place. The challenge for educational reformers the world over is two-fold. First, we all need to get better at (and a bit more humble about) identifying the best program elements from the entire community of practice. Quite likely, no single one of us has gotten everything right. However, taken together, we likely have many of the necessary components for a good solution. Second, we need better processes for connecting these various ideas into a holistic solution that can—and herein lies the tension—be adapted and customized for each location (school, district, city, region, or country).

This need for customization and coordination leads us to our third theme: there is a fundamental tension between impact and scale. We assert that the resolution of that tension will take at least three generations of students in a society, and no amount of effort or investment can accelerate that resolution. Harking back to Oscar Becerra, social change is "neither magic nor fast." Thus, we need to commit to the long, slow march of cultural adaptation. For all that can be done to improve, refine, and standardize the building blocks that form the core program elements of any education reform effort, the most important factor in the success of educational change is local commitment. With time and great effort, these building blocks can be adapted and structured for the local context; and with additional investments of time and money, we can begin building local commitment and improve local capacity.

The model by which all of us working in the education sector have achieved our early progress and impact is neither fully scalable nor sustainable. And the greatest risk to that sustainability is that progress is measured too soon, and the return on investment deemed too small. Our wager is that, as difficult as it is to start and sustain these local efforts, education is societally cumulative—the better educated this generation, the easier it will be to educate the next generation. Education reform will only become entrenched in the third generation. That is forty-five to sixty years out! School reform *will* finally occur when a generation of children whose expectations about learning are vastly different are themselves in the driver's seat. In other words, it will come from the bottom up. As a movement, we have to both figure out the interim measures and incremental successes that we can celebrate to maintain momentum and improve our ability to coordinate efforts so that change can grow to national, and eventually global, scale.

Learning about Social Innovation and Social Entrepreneurship

Too often, the terms "social innovator" and "social entrepreneur" are used interchangeably, and yet we see them as two fundamentally different roles and activities, both of which are vital for driving solutions to our endemic social problems. The distinction between the two is also essential for understanding OLPC. Innovation—whether social or otherwise—is fundamentally about improvement based on experimentation, inventing wholly new things or processes or putting existing things together in new ways that create value. Entrepreneurship, on the other hand, need not include innovation; it is about packaging and selling a "product"—again, whether a widget or a social program—and taking on the risk associated with starting and running an enterprise.

At OLPC, we initially envisioned ourselves as pure innovators. Hence our theory of action depended on entrepreneurs in the market embracing the vision that OLPC demonstrated—the possibility of creating a laptop custom designed to meet the learning needs of children in the developing world and using this as a tool to revolutionize education—and themselves running with it to create enterprises and absorb the risk. Our upfront investments in innovation depended on the actions of others for them to realize any impact. We did not start out with the assumption that we would ourselves be entrepreneurs; indeed, we were wholly unqualified for this particular challenge. However, the lack of market adoption of our ideas—by private companies, NGOs, or governments—forced us to become social entrepreneurs. We had invested so much in the development of the XO and Sugar, and we were so clear that our vision was both right and possible, that we felt committed to expand our efforts to include the manufacturing, distribution, sales, and support.

Extending beyond our core areas of competency has created myriad difficulties for us over the years and, we think, is in no small part the source of much of the pointed, and largely correct, criticisms we have encountered. And yet, as we look across the social sector, we are comforted by realizing that we are not alone in our experience; given our brand recognition and vocal presence on the international stage, we were, perhaps, simply uniquely visible as we struggled, failed, and occasionally succeeded in learning. Social innovators of all stripes—whether from education, public health, urban development, environmental science, or other sectors—will often have a fabulous technical and human solution to a social problem. They may be on to something that truly works in changing the life experience of their beneficiaries or the lived experience of a community! And yet, to take their idea to scale and ensure that they are changing the world at any degree of scale, they will—like us—need an entrepreneurial and business-minded skill set that very few bring to the table initially. In other words, to drive impact at scale, we all need to be—or become—both social innovators and social entrepreneurs.

The Unique Challenges of Product-Driven Social Innovation

Many of the organizations that are best known in the social sector focus on scaling human services solutions to social problems; hence the popularity of programs such as the Peace Corps or AmeriCorps, which are fundamentally about providing dedicated, motivated (and low-cost) human resources to devote themselves to social problems. OLPC stands with a very few organizations as a product-driven organization of social change (other examples include such organizations as KickStart, which provides low-cost irrigation solutions for agriculture in developing countries, or SolarAid, which is pioneering the creation of solar-charged devices to work around the challenges of inconsistent energy availability). When there is a "thing" that must be created at the center of your social solution, becoming an effective entrepreneur becomes even more important.

There is a popular euphemism in business that ideas are cheap and execution is hard. Put another way, the last 10 percent of the road from idea to impact represents 90 percent of the work. For a product-driven social innovator, the chain extends from idea to *product* to impact. This has a number of implications. In the creation of a product, it is likely, if not certain, that you will be engaged in a cross-sector effort to create a supply chain from idea to product that includes private-sector partners who are engaged in the process of manufacture and distribution of your product. Hence, the ability to see, understand, and balance the incentives of multiple different types of organizational entities is vital, and recognizing from the outset that private enterprises may have less flexibility inherent in their business models is important. Additionally, there will be organizational commitments to manage along the value chain from product to impact. In the case of product-based social entrepreneurship—where the cost of developing a concept or idea into a product is high—and you often cannot drive any on-the-ground impact without this essential input—it becomes that much more important that real purchase commitments emerge and that a solid execution plan be in place. As our experiences illustrate, understanding these constraints and planning for them in advance may help you to avoid some of the bumps in the road and organizational emergencies that emerged for us in our naïveté.

Always Certain, Sometimes Right

There is another lesson regarding social innovation and social entrepreneurship that we think the social sector—in particular in the United States—is just beginning to appreciate: the importance of field-systems innovation and entrepreneurship or, put differently, of connecting and linking ideas. Innovation rarely occurs in such a way that it does not call into question the value or efficiency of existing solutions. At OLPC, we were certain in our beliefs. And in our arrogance, we often considered the efforts and results of others to be subpar. In doing so, we missed out on potential opportunities to create the partnerships necessary to achieve scale and sustainability.

While you should never excuse performance below expectations, those same organizations whose work and effort may appear to you misguided may have resources that can be marshaled and redirected if you can convince them to cooperate. "Stand with me" is much more inviting than "Get to the back of the line." And while building alliances consumes time and resources and, in forming partnerships, your original vision will be buffeted and shaped by more opinions, the investment will pay off in terms of the advantages of scale, perspective, and reach that the right partnerships can bring.

Finding a Balance between Seeing What You Believe and Believing What You See

Innovators are by their nature visionaries who must simultaneously protect and promote their ideas until they are strong enough to stand on their own. Social innovators are perhaps even more protective and passionate because their efforts are in the service of the public good rather than that of personal gain. That mindset of protection and promotion is served well by seeing what you believe: finding ways to make the world fit your models and ideas. But as your only lens on the world, seeing what you believe can be dangerous. Social innovators (and enterprises) must be able to protect and promote a vision while being open to the possibility that our underlying assumptions about the theory of change or theory of action might be incorrect. Counter-factual data or contrary opinions are a powerful force for validation and improvement if they are not being filtered out by the overwhelming motivation to protect and promote.

At OLPC, we believed so strongly in our work that there was never a question of stopping. But that passion blinded us to the scope of work for which we eventually assumed responsibility. We did not acknowledge the all-or-nothing nature of some of our decisions, e.g., manufacturing a laptop and writing a software platform. We took on roles we had expected the market to perform, often under the continued belief that our role was only to inspire and catalyze the market. We believed that the market would eventually catch on and catch up, that it would literally take the business away from us. At the same time, we were so invested in our own products that we were reluctant to let go. In truth, the market sent us a very different message: that our path, while righteous and important, was too dangerous and uncertain for for-profit companies to travel. We learned that a shared vision for partnership and impact can be undone by the failure of parties to understand one another's motivations and appetite for risk. The for-profit market is a powerful force to be harnessed for social change, but do not assume you can change what motivates the market and do not assume that the private sector thinks like you do, even if you share the same aspirations.

Learning about Being Part of a Social Movement

At the Battle of Mobile Bay during the American Civil War, Rear Admiral David Farragut is alleged to have said, "Damn the torpedoes, full

SEVEN SECRETS

When he was director of the MIT Media Lab, Walter Bender published a brief statement of the "seven secrets" that made the lab such a unique and powerful source of innovative ideas across sectors. These secrets are relevant for all those who desire to "think differently" and make a difference.

1. The sun is evocative of a light shining into every corner: No dark corners; an unfettered exchange of ideas; pooled intellectual property; no barriers between partners and the work.

2. The phases of the moon represent the cyclical process of innovation: "Imagine and realize." Have an idea and build a prototype—engage in authentic, critical dialog—iterate. Learn from mistakes and successes.

3. Fire signifies fuel: Invest in the passion of people, not their projects. It is the fire that burns inside a person that will result in change.

4. Water brings to mind Plato's interpretation of Heraclitus: "You cannot step twice in the same river." Change is the only constant; do not get tied to any approach; incorporate emerging ideas and jettison tired ones.

5. Wood is used as a metaphor for design and engineering, which need to be comingled.

6. Gold to be mined comes from the collision of ideas—interdisciplinary community, which expresses itself through critical dialog, is how lead is turned into gold.

7. We ground ourselves in real problems and take risks.

speed ahead." Sometimes it feels precisely right to keep moving forward, ignoring warning signs and naysayers. However, we have learned that there is a tension between forging ahead with a revolutionary idea and slowing down to ensure that the community of practice keeps pace with you. Recall Negroponte telling countries that were not willing to ante up for one million laptops to "get to the back of the line."

Challenging (and, to some, inspiring) words. And yet, for most of the types of entrenched problems we face, there will never be a declared victory. When the euphoria of the initial phases of the revolution fades, and the protracted and entrenched battle is underway, it's nice to have allies.

Going it alone can create immediate impact, and it pretty much ensures that your voice and your vision hold true. But taking the time to engage a broader community of actors to garner their support and absorb their critique may ultimately enable you to create better impact and drive both scale and sustainability. The better-impact argument is simply that the ideas are vetted and improved by a wider audience of engaged thinkers. Joy's Law—a popular aphorism in the high-tech industry—suggests that "No matter who you are, most of the smartest people work for someone else." Attributed to Sun Microsystems cofounder Bill Joy, this "law" emphasizes the importance of building bridges between organizations. The essential knowledge problem that faces many enterprises today is that, in any given sphere of activity, much of the pertinent knowledge will reside outside the boundaries of any one organization. The central challenge for those who aim for significant change or innovation is to find ways to access that knowledge.[3] OLPC did a great job of engaging a broad community of thinkers in building both the hardware and the software. However, when it came to implementation and ensuring that we build out a program that would truly drive the educational and learning goals we had in focus, there was much less effort invested—and sometimes significant resistance.

A Final Thought

It is impossible to say where OLPC would be today if we had taken a different path. We put the children we are working to help at the center of our efforts and have focused on studying and improving what we have accomplished. Until recently, we have invested little time in exploring the "what ifs." What is important, however, is the future. We have learned that complex multidimensional problems will not get solved in just one way, or even with one set of solutions, and definitely not by one organization. OLPC is evolving as an organization into a movement that balances the need to create meaningful and direct impact for children with the engagement of the broader community of learning to identify models for even greater impact through partnership and addressing the root causes of the problems we care about. Going forward, engaging our partners in our efforts is an important metric for the success of our organization. We end with the words of Eben Moglen, founder of the Software Freedom Law Center:

> I am moved by the experience of becoming merely one among many—another of the minds and hands drawn to the work of inventing a better world.

APPENDIX A

CAMBODIA, A DECADE LATER

WHEN NICHOLAS NEGROPONTE CHOSE THE SITE FOR the school he and his then wife, Elaine, would fund and build in Cambodia, he did so from on high, quite literally. In 1999, Negroponte used what was at the time the only helicopter in Cambodia's air force (which later crashed) to take a tour of the countryside. He chose a location that, looking down, he estimated to be close enough to a number of nearby villages that there would be sufficient students to fill a school. That location was Reaksmy Commune, Preah Vihear Province, the site of the school that has been cited time and again in the telling of the origins of OLPC.

In stark contrast to Negroponte's larger-than-life persona is his now ex-wife, Elaine. Soft-spoken, sincere, and rigorously avoiding the spotlight, Elaine Negroponte describes herself as someone who pays attention to details. She has spent six months out of every year in Cambodia in the fourteen years since Nicholas Negroponte pointed down at the hillside in Reaksmy. She has been the driving force behind Cambodia PRIDE (Providing Rural Innovative Digital Education), a small, independent 501(c)(3) non-profit organization that is the ongoing legacy of the original experiments in using computer technology for education in Cambodia.[1] The stated goal of PRIDE is "to encourage students' independent thinking and problem solving, with the goal of improving their quality of life."

Until 2011, the project in Cambodia that was the original inspiration for OLPC, and which Elaine Negroponte has continued to drive, had not been formally associated with OLPC. As of the writing of this book, PRIDE is in discussions with OLPC about the possibility of becoming a Type II supporting organization to OLPC; in essence this is a "brother-sister" relationship, in which the goals and operations of the two entities will be linked in a specified manner.[2] Although not formally part of OLPC at present, the work in Cambodia is as legitimate a test of the power and possibility of OLPC's mission and vision as any of the projects with which the organization is formally associated, and it is one of the best examples of an attempt to drive impact in a primarily rural, and shockingly poor, society.

EDUCATIONAL NEED IN CAMBODIA

Cambodia has a complicated and bloody history, even in recent decades. The country suffered dramatic losses due to spillover of conflict during the Vietnam War; rice fields were destroyed and crops lost, domestic animals used for farming and food were killed en masse, and the population of male Cambodians was drastically depleted.

Of Cambodia's population, approximately one-third live in poverty, and by far the majority of these are in rural areas. Historically, education in Cambodia was offered by Buddhist pagodas (*wats*), which meant that only males could attend school. During the time of the Khmer Rouge, most educated members of society—including teachers, monks, and anyone who could read—were killed by the government. In the post-Khmer Rouge Cambodian constitution written in 1993, free and mandatory education for all Cambodians for nine years is guaranteed, essentially supporting a universal right to basic education. Despite this, overall access to and quality of education is highly variable in the country. As Elaine Negroponte explains, "The population of children is huge. You could build a school every other day. And that's not their problem: they have plenty of schools, but don't have any teachers." Especially in rural areas of the country—many of which are fairly isolated given Cambodia's distinctive geography—the quality of schools and teachers tends to be quite low. To say that the educational system is inadequate in most places is a drastic understatement.

Elaine Negroponte's description of her experience in the schools when she first began spending time in Reaksmy is particularly evocative: "At the primary school, the typical teacher's work day is: arrive late, take attendance to have a record that they came to work, sit under a tree for a while and then leave early." The results of this broken system are profound: "No one in these [rural] villages [goes] anywhere. It's really hard to get them through junior high, never mind high school. There's no tomorrow." A key part of the education challenge then, and one that is less often recognized, is ensuring that the practical, everyday value of education—relative to other use of time—is clear.

THE ENN SCHOOL

The original impetus for building schools in Cambodia came not from Elaine and Nicholas Negroponte, but from a friend and colleague of theirs, Bernie

Krisher, the MIT Media Lab's Tokyo liaison. Krisher was working with a World Bank program called American Assistance to Cambodia to build schools in the country and asked the Negropontes if they would support the building of one of the first schools.

The ENN School (named after Elaine and Nicholas) was the second school to be built through this program. For a cost of only $10,000, a brick-and-mortar school was constructed, and Krisher's organization provided both a solar panel to power one desktop computer and a teacher to provide instruction in both English and computer-learning programs. The school was completed in 1999, and Nicholas, Elaine, and their son Dimitri went to the opening. In 2000, Dimitri Negroponte returned to help set up and run the school and to serve as the English and computer-programming teacher. Nicholas Negroponte and Krisher negotiated a deal with Thaksin Shinawatra—then prime minister of Thailand—to provide a satellite dish and local Wifi. With this deal, the school in Reaksmy was among the first to have Internet access, which was—and remains to this date—free of charge.

In 2010, Cambodia PRIDE worked with 168 primary school students and 285 secondary school students (the latter made up of students from surrounding villages), with a staff of two and a budget of $25,000, most of which was donated by Elaine Negroponte herself. It is a minuscule project by many standards, but with much to teach OLPC and the world about what it takes to drive tangible impact on students in supporting learning and expanding life opportunities.

THE VIEW FROM THE GROUND IN REAKSMY

Cambodia PRIDE evolved from a program that aimed to provide laptops and Internet access to primary-school children, into a program that works with both primary- and secondary-school students, using technology as a tool to help them to develop essential practical skills. As Elaine Negroponte explains: "I like to say we are a little Montessori and a lot vocational training, which I'm afraid OLPC usually cringes at."

Showing Up is Half the Battle

Perhaps the simplest factor driving the success of the PRIDE program is its consistency. "If a small child goes several times to school walking from a far distance away and finds that the room is locked or there is no teacher—that child leaves and does not come back to school." The PRIDE program, in contrast, is run consistently eight hours a day from Monday through Friday. Students can count on a qualified teacher who is present in the classroom and an opportunity to engage and learn.

Drop and Run Doesn't Work

The first challenge was getting the technology up and running. The original technology setup for the school included one computer, a solar panel, a small satellite dish (VSAT), and wireless Internet. When Dimitri Negroponte came to the school, he brought with him a number of Panasonic ToughBooks—army spec and virtually indestructible—that had been donated by Panasonic to the program. Later, OLPC donated fifteen hundred XO laptops that were distributed to primary school students in Reaksmy (and some of which were shared with other schools in Cambodia). As Elaine Negroponte explains, "OLPC initially thought 'Couldn't the laptops just be dropped off?' But it's just not going to work. There's no power—that's your first hurdle."[3]

Teachers Matter

A second challenge was ensuring that the technology was used for learning. It quickly became clear that, given the overall quality of teaching in Cambodia, and in particular in rural areas, relying upon Cambodian staff to understand technology and integrate it into their approach to teaching was unrealistic in the short term, and perhaps in the long term as well. As Elaine Negroponte says, "There was a big block between technology and teachers for many reasons. They were suspicious of this machine that had somehow invaded and was possibly taking a lot of the attention of the student. They wondered, where is this going, and what is my place in this?"[4]

The decision Negroponte has made, then, has been to staff the technology and English-learning programs with Cambodian teachers and to have a consistent pattern of visiting Westerners who run periodic workshops to inspire and provide new ideas for teachers and students alike. In addition to providing a dedicated teacher to support the technology and English programs, PRIDE works very closely with classroom teachers to help them to understand, and to use, the technology being provided to students.

Integrate Technology into a Practical Curriculum

In the early days of experiments with using laptops for learning, the importance of integrating technology into the existing school curriculum was consistently downplayed. As Negroponte explains, there was "no conversation in the early days about curriculum. In talking with people like Professor Seymour Papert, the word 'curriculum' always made them cringe." However, in Reaksmy, it became very important to student learning that the technology become an integrated part of the curriculum of learning in the schools.

When the school first started—and with the country still recovering from civil upheaval—the government allowed all students, no matter how old, to return to school. The result was classes with younger and older students mixed together—a real challenge for a both teacher and student. As Negroponte explains, technology ironically became a tool for managing this diversity; using a computer in any class means that students can learn at their own pace without any stigma related to age. This helped to accelerate acceptance of the computers by both students and teachers and made a case for having the technology in the classroom.

The XO laptops are used by all students in the primary school as general learning tools to support the standard Khmer school curriculum; PRIDE also supports a supplemental English-learning program. For all programs, the teaching and learning approach is truly hands-on, encouraging students to explore and create for themselves. As Elaine explains, this approach is revolutionary compared to the standard educational approach: "This is the first time these kids are creating something for themselves. Ever. It gives them a whole different way to see the world and imagine themselves in it."

Create a Through Line to Secondary School

A really important development in Reaksmy was the extension of learning support for students beyond the traditional OLPC focus on younger, primary-school students. By ensuring that every primary school student had a laptop, a problem emerged when they hit junior high school. Whereas primary schools typically are located in one village, secondary schools—due to resource constraints and drop-out rates as students age—typically are made up of students from multiple villages. When students from Reaksmy went to secondary school, they started encountering others from villages that had not had training in computers or English; a stratification into haves and have-nots started to emerge and created tensions.

To combat the emerging stratification, tip the cost-benefit in favor of school, and sustain the early learning of primary-school students, Negroponte and her team quickly recognized that it was vital to support student learning once they left primary school. The difficulty, however, was how to do so in a world of constrained resources—their innovation was to set up an XO lending library; the students who received the XOs in primary school still have theirs, whereas students from other villages can check out an XO for their own use.

It's a Community Program, not a Technology Initiative

In looking at the realities of the current PRIDE program in Reaksmy, one is struck most powerfully by the fact that while technology is central to the teaching and learning experience, the success of the program seems to hinge on an intimacy of relationship that has evolved between the program and the community. Elaine and the teachers know these students and their families well, down to the details of family economics, family violence in their homes, and their struggle with decisions about whether and how to keep their children in school. The key insight for the program was noting the need to provide supports that attend to factors outside the classroom that might prevent attendance and performance, as well as to pay attention to the overall well-being of the students.[5]

WHAT IMPACT LOOKS LIKE IN REAKSMY

The first students to benefit from the PRIDE program are only now graduating from high school. In fact, two of the women from this first class are studying computer science in a nearby two-year college. As Negroponte explains, this is a huge shift: "People for the first time in these villages are going on to higher education and are learning what it means to stay in school."

As with many social-change initiatives, gauging impact in a manner more systematic than collecting anecdotes of individual student experiences is difficult in Reaksmy. A real challenge is agreeing on what success might be in this context. "I would never want to shift them away from being farmers. Being rice farmers is important, especially in a place like Cambodia. More than education, it's about making decisions, making choices, and deciding what's best." The focus, then, is perhaps not on meeting hard measures of accomplishment—high-school completion or attainment of a college degree—but on expanding the time horizon for decision making and the sense of possibility each student brings to his or her life. In some sense, the project really focuses on empowering students and building their sense of self.

APPENDIX B

DRIVING CHANGE
FROM THE TOP

OLPC IN PERU AND URUGUAY

A S A NATURAL CONSEQUENCE OF OUR ORIGINAL FOCUS on "handshake" deals with heads of state to launch OLPC projects, top-down initiatives coordinated through the central government and Ministry of Education were among our earliest deployments. Two such projects—in Peru and in Uruguay—highlight both the similarities and the challenges that result from taking a top-down approach to education reform in very different geographic and social contexts.

PERU

Peru is a country of juxtapositions. Geographically it is one of the most diverse equatorial countries on the planet, with arid coastal plains, vast Amazonian rainforests, and snow-covered Andean peaks within its borders. Socially, Peru is a complex mix of Spanish and indigenous cultures. Economically, the coastal regions have relatively high levels of wealth and social and economic development, while the majority of the population lives in deep poverty, unconnected to social mobility and development along the coast; the population of the mountainous—and difficult to reach—central regions lives in deep poverty, largely unconnected to and unreachable by the outside world.

With these vast disparities, Peru is a country so seemingly challenging that we did not originally consider it a viable target country for an OLPC project. Consequently, the energy to bring OLPC to Peru was born in Peru. The principal champion was Oscar Becerra, a former IBM executive who worked in the Ministry of Education. Becerra needed to find a universal solution to three broad problems in the education system. First, he saw what he describes as meaningless formal education, with "lots of how's, but very few why's." As he explains: "I had always been convinced the main problem with formal education was its lack of meaning for the student that is answering the question 'Why should I learn what you expect me to learn and are trying to teach?'" Children did not understand why they were being told to learn what they needed to learn; that drove many children to determine that it was better to help out at home than to waste their time in school. Second, the quality of teachers was poor. In the spring of 2008, 185,000 teachers in Peru took an exam to apply for teaching positions in the public education system. Only 5 percent of teachers passed the test and only 151 scored high enough to earn tenure. Third, the structure and crowding of most classrooms made individual attention non-existent.[1] Becerra saw OLPC as an opportunity for Peru to solve his three critical challenges through both the technology of the laptop and the constructionist approach embedded into Sugar.

In July 2007 Education Minister José Antonio Chang announced that Peru would participate in the OLPC project. The plan at the time was to start with 150,000 XOs to be distributed to children and teachers in 6,000 rural schoolhouses. Additionally, they ran a contest for the distribution of another 100,000 XOs in urban schools, with the winner chosen based on a competition for the best proposal. Carla Gómez Monroy, a veteran of multiple OLPC deployments, set up a pilot program at a one-room, multi-grade school in Arahuay, a village selected by Becerra, in the mountains, approximately 100 kilometers to the northeast of Lima. The school, Institución Educativa Apóstol Santiago, is a combination primary and secondary school, 2,600 meters above sea level. It is so remote that mobile phones need a special antenna to receive a signal. In a nod to future aspirations rather than current reality, Becerra had chosen a location that could have an antenna installed for Internet access. Almost every parent attended the launch ceremony, walking long distances to the school.

The Arahuay pilot was intended to simulate the expected deployment conditions of a typical rural deployment. Training was limited for both students and teachers—it focused on the basics of getting the machine up and running, with the expectation that the people themselves would figure out how to use it and that learning would be improved organically. Such a model was critical to Peru's ability to support a national roll-out—the program simply would not work if intensive or ongoing training was required. Employing an arguably risky strategy, the ministry empowered children and their teachers to find their own way to use the laptop to improve education. In parallel, the ministry worked on improving teacher capabilities and support over a longer time frame. In Arahuay, Gómez Monroy ensured that there was a large degree of community and parental involvement, although that was not necessarily the case in every school in the broader roll-out.

The Arahuay results were positive—teachers were reporting increased communication between children in and out of class, increased sharing of ideas, and a change in family perception of school. Based on these results, OLPC developed a "deployment guide" that covered planning, execution, and support, along with tips, sample documents, and a glossary of OLPC terms. The Associated Press, reporting on Arahuay, said: "Doubts about whether poor, rural children really can benefit from quirky little computers evaporate as quickly as the morning dew in this hilltop Andean village, where 50 primary school children got machines from the One Laptop Per Child project six months ago."[2]

The immediate impact of the Arahuay pilot was enough for Becerra and Chang to gain critical support from President Alan García Pérez for the project. But they also knew that García Pérez's support would not be enough; to get the necessary capital for expansion, they needed the support of the Ministry of Finance as well. Becerra worked with the Peruvian Congress to secure financing for the OLPC project, and Congress also authorized a competitive bid process for which OLPC was well positioned given that specifications closely matched the OLPC program. Congress removed significant uncertainty from the deal by securing the funding through legislative action in October 2007, and, in so doing, it ensured the security of the purchase price for Peru. This meant that the ball had begun rolling; the order for the first 150,000 machines could be approved.

Looking beyond Arahuay, the basic plan was to leverage 143 regional distribution centers (UGELs)—already in place for tasks such as the distribution of textbooks—as the primary mechanism for supporting the schools. Many of the targeted schools are multiple travel days from the UGELs; 93 percent of the schools were initially without Internet access and 10 percent had no electricity. To complement the support at the UGELs, the ministry, with help from OLPC, established several internship programs with the goal of sending support teams directly to the schools. In addition, teachers were brought in to four regional centers for a week-long introduction to the technology and, more important, instruction in how to use the laptop for learning.

The Peru deployment has not been without its critics. In a January 2012 Brookings Institute report, Rebecca Winthrop, director of the Center for Universal Education did not pull any punches:

In Peru, a number of colorful laptops sit in a corner of a classroom covered with dust. Given to the school through a One Laptop Per Child program arranged by the Ministry of Education, the laptops were intended to improve students' information communication technology (ICT) skills, as well as their content-related skills. Without the proper support for teacher training in how the laptops are used, with no follow-up or repair and maintenance contingencies, and with outdated and bug-infested software, the laptops are seen as unusable and serve little purpose. In this case, technology has not helped improve the educational experience of learners.[3]

In a deployment as large as that in Peru, there is bound to be variance in terms of quality. And while laptops do not gather dust in most schools, there is some truth to Winthrop's characterizations. The situation in Peru is exacerbated by the formidable challenges posed by its geography. The disconnect between the capital and the school network remains the core issue and has ripple effects across the program: Maintenance and repair of the laptops does not occur at the level needed, ongoing teacher training and support are difficult, and the teachers themselves are not able to connect with one another to fill the gap.

Despite these challenges, Peru's support for the OLPC program has remained consistent and has, in fact, grown. As it has unfolded, the Arahuay pilot was the first step down a path that has resulted in nearly one million XOs being shipped to Peru to date.

URUGUAY

In stark contrast to the challenges faced in Peru, Uruguay can be held up as an example of how OLPC's original vision of providing laptop computers to children can be realized. The country was, by many measures, an ideal candidate for OLPC's mission and ideas. With a population of 3.5 million residents, of whom an estimated 400,000 are children between the ages of six and twelve, providing a laptop to each child in Uruguay, though ambitious, was within reach.

Despite its favorable educational history, in 2005 Uruguay was in critical need of improving educational outcomes and enhancing the preparedness of its young people—in particular low-income youth—for the labor market. Despite universal free education, in 2007 the net enrollment rate among twelve- to fourteen-year-olds was 68 percent, and only 39 percent among fifteen- to seventeen-year-olds. A high number of students, mostly from the poorest households, dropped out at ages thirteen or fourteen, in the transition from primary to secondary school. In the 2006 Program for International

Student Assessment (PISA) exam, an international student achievement test that gauges the scholastic performance of fifteen-year-old students, Uruguay placed first in the region in mathematics and second in reading and science; yet, of all the countries participating in the test, Uruguay also had one of the greatest standard deviations among schools, suggesting significant variability by socioeconomic level.[4]

In March of 2005, Uruguay ushered in its first socialist government with the new president, Tabaré Vázquez. The political environment was ripe for grand ideas and decisive action. On November 16, 2005, a delegation from Uruguay watched Nicholas Negroponte unveil the prototype of the $100 laptop at the United Nations' World Summit on the Information Society (WSIS) in Tunis. The concept of providing one laptop per child captured the imagination of the leadership of Uruguay. The idea that the government could begin bridging the "digital divide"—so emblematic of social inequality—through OLPC seemed to President Vázquez precisely the innovation that could enable him to fulfill his campaign promise and bring Uruguay to regional prominence.

In December 2006, Vázquez announced the launch of Plan Ceibal—Conectividad Educativa de Informática Básica para el Aprendizaje en Línea (which can be translated as "Educational Connectivity and Basic Computing for On-line Learning")—headed by Miguel Brechner to provide not just laptops but also Internet connectivity to every primary-school student and their teachers. This latter goal was facilitated by a plan to install an extensive grid of cellphone and DSL services connected through fiber optics throughout the country.

In May 2007, Vázquez inaugurated a pilot project of 150 laptops in the rural town of Villa Cardal in the Department of Florida (about 80 kilometers from the capital); this was to become the first primary school in Uruguay in which all children and their teachers would have an XO.

In August of 2007, about three months into the pilot experience, Juan Pablo Hourcade, from the University of Iowa, Diana Beitler from the London School of Economics, Fernando Cormenzana, of NEXT Consulting, and Pablo Flores, from the Universidad de la República, visited the school and carried out a qualitative evaluation of the pilot. The evaluation indicated that students' motivation for reading and writing had increased, since the laptops gave them access to a wider set of reading materials and the opportunity to share their writing with others through the school's blog. At home, children taught their parents and siblings how to use the laptops. Parents used the laptops for a range of needs from looking up information (e.g., such as maps) to more complex activities such as coordinating milk pick-ups from their dairy farms.[5]

The evaluation also noted that connectivity was a challenge, especially when the children were not at school. There were also serious problems with input devices; for example, many of the laptops' touchpads were not working well, and about one in five laptops were being repaired due to problems with their keyboards. Finally, the evaluation noted that the software that came with the laptops was not particularly child-friendly. The evaluators noted the need for larger icons, translated user interfaces, file browsers that are more easily used by children, and localized themes and content (e.g., author music with popular rhythms).[6] It is worth noting that, based in large part on feedback from Uruguay, many changes and improvements have been made to both the XO and Sugar, including new touchpad and keyboard designs and many new Sugar features and enhancements.

In 2010, Plan Ceibal was morphed into its own, newly created organization: the Center for Technological and Social Inclusion (CITS). As of late 2011, the approximately 180 employees at CITS worked on all aspects of Plan Ceibal: evaluating hardware; designing network solutions; training teachers; developing educational content; and evaluating the educational and social impact of the initiative. Gómez Monroy who set up many of the pilot deployments for OLPC, articulated what might be the single most important insight into OLPC's accomplishments in Uruguay to date: the deployment she said, was "a top-down initiative, turned a bottom-up movement."[7] Indeed, a whole ecosystem of organizations and leaders from the public, private, and civil society sectors have emerged to fulfill a variety of roles in implementing, maintaining, improving, complementing, evaluating, learning from, and communicating Plan Ceibal and its work.[8]

In July 2007, two months after initiating the first pilot, the government of Uruguay issued a request for proposal (RFP) that solicited 100,000 laptops to be delivered in a series of stages. The RFP encompassed requirements of software, school servers, connectivity devices, and support and maintenance. It mentions that "teachers will be trained in the use of these tools and the development of new educational proposals."[9] The RFP specifies that the first pilot will be in the Department of Florida and will *include all children and teachers in all public elementary schools.* It will bring connectivity to all the schools and to as many local homes as possible. Less than three years after issuing the RFP, all public primary schools in Uruguay had laptops for both students and teachers; today it is not unusual to see a group of children sitting outdoors, laptops open, learning.

On March 1, 2010, José Mujica was sworn in as the new president of Uruguay, replacing Vázquez and extending the leadership of the Frente Amplio Party. Mujica has continued to implement and expand many of the policies of the Vázquez administration, a good sign for the future of OLPC in Uruguay.

APPENDIX C

OLPC AMERICA

I N JANUARY 2008, OLPC ANNOUNCED THAT WE PLANNED TO set up a separate entity focusing on the United States—OLPC America—as part of an ongoing strategy to use "first world" markets to help fund "third world" markets. This was part of the same line of thinking that generated the Give One, Get One Campaign.

To date, OLPC has deployed tens of thousands of XO laptops in classrooms, schools, districts, and cities in the United States in an eclectic set of projects. These include urban deployments such as Teaching Matters, a foundation working in the New York City public schools. Rural deployments include the Big Sky Science Partnership, which is bringing XO laptops into the classrooms of elementary teachers on and near the Crow and Northern Cheyenne Reservations in Montana. There are also examples of projects that realize the "developed-developing country exchange" envisioned for OLPC America, such as the Fargo-to-Sudan Project, which is working to import the after-school program at Madison Elementary School in to schools in southern Sudan. For the most part, projects and deployments in the United States have tended to result from the activities of a strong local champion: a maverick teacher or an ambitious administrator.

BIRMINGHAM

In December 2007, the mayor of Birmingham, Alabama, Larry Langford, announced that his city would be the first in the United States to provide one laptop for each student in the public primary schools in the city. "We live in a digital age, so it is important that all our children have equal access to technology and are able to integrate it into all aspects of their lives. We are proud that

Birmingham is on its way to eliminating the so-called 'digital divide' and to ensuring that our children have state-of-the-art tools for education."

With a surrounding metropolitan area population of more than one million, the city of Birmingham is the largest city in Alabama (and home to nearly one-quarter of the state's total population). The city itself has a population of more than two hundred thousand, of which almost 75 percent self-identified as black on the 2010 US census. Birmingham is an industrial center and serves as a transportation crossroads, but is best known for the national attention it drew during the civil rights movement of the 1950s and '60s as the site of some of the more notorious acts of violence, including the bombing of the Sixteenth Street Baptist Church.

The Birmingham school system, run by the Birmingham Board of Education, has a student population of more than thirty thousand children, and includes forty-one elementary and primary schools. The greater metropolitan area is home to numerous independent school districts, some of which have a national reputation for quality. However, the schools in the inner city share many of the problems of poor urban districts throughout the country: low achievement, poor attendance, and poor graduation rates. In 2006 Alabama ranked forty-fourth in the nation (out of fifty states) in high school graduation, with only an estimated 66 percent of students completing high school (significantly below the national average of 75 percent).[1]

In 2008 Mayor Langford used his executive power to purchase 15,500 XO laptops (at a price tag of $200 each), with the intention of implementing an OLPC program in the city's schools in the coming year. This decision represented a nearly $3 million expenditure on the part of Birmingham city schools. To put this purchase into context, in 2008 Alabama ranked thirty-fourth (out of fifty states) in spending per pupil; the Birmingham school district had an annual budget of approximately $350 million, with an average expenditure per pupil of $12,400.[2] For some, this additional $200 per primary school student seemed like small stakes given the potential payoff; for others, it raised real concerns. However, during the 2008–2009 school year, first- through fifth-grade students and teachers in all public primary schools in Birmingham received XO laptops.

From the beginning, the deployment of these laptops faced some daunting challenges. Langford's decision had been taken unilaterally, making it unpopular among members of the Board of Education and the teachers and administrators charged with implementing the program (there was a prevailing sense of disempowerment). In addition, it was recognized early on that there was a deficit in the provision of the Internet to schools, which would be a barrier to the laptops being used as recommended by OLPC, and that remedying the situation would be costly. Further, many teachers were not interested in monitoring Internet use in their classrooms, so the lack of access was not seen as a high priority within the system. In the wake of the debacle in the formal education sector, the informal sector stepped in. When the school system made a unilateral decision not to provide Internet access to the children, an unanticipated but positive response emerged from the Birmingham Public Library, which offered to provide supervised access, along with laptop-related activities, in all its twenty-one branches across the metropolitan area. A number of church groups did something similar, providing a location in which interested students could work with—and learn using—the laptops. Another problem solved outside of the system was repairs. A local group teamed up with OLPC to establish an autonomous Birmingham repair center, independent of City Hall and the school district.

The impact of the XO laptops in Birmingham has been the subject of much debate. Shelia Cotten, a sociologist at the University of Alabama–Birmingham, published a study in 2010 in which she noted that the impact of the XO on students varied in conjunction with the extent of their teacher's use of the XO; those students whose teachers used the XO in the classroom were more likely to use their own XOs and to show that the XO positively impacted their learning.[3] In a 2012 follow-up study exploring ongoing patterns of usage of the XO, Cotten, with Mark Warschauer of the University of California, Irvine, and Morgan Ames of Stanford University, reported that most students used their XOs very little at school and that many encountered technical problems: the XOs broke down and couldn't be repaired by students. The authors asserted that "the XO is not really teacher-friendly" since it has a small keyboard and display; that teacher training in use of the laptop is insufficient; and that the lack of an external video port prevents teachers from effectively integrating it into their classroom teaching. They concluded: "Any educational reform effort with digital media needs to be grounded in solid curricular and pedagogical foundations, include requisite social and technical support, and be carried out with detailed planning, monitoring, and evaluation."[4]

We agree with the importance of engaging and training teachers and ensuring that maintenance and support of the machines is available. We too have observed that successful OLPC deployments have evolved a "learning ecosystem" to enable all of these requirements, as well as others not mentioned. What Cotten and others point to, correctly, is the learning curve that OLPC has been traversing in regard to what it takes to deploy and fully support the XO in service of driving student learning.[5]

CROTON-ON-HUDSON

In sharp contrast to the experience in Birmingham is a deployment at the Pierre Van Cortland Middle School in the 8,000-person town of Croton-on-Hudson, New York. Launched in 2008 by Dr. Gerald Ardito—a science teacher at the school—the program works with 150 fifth-grade students and their teachers. Ardito is a strong proponent of self-directed learning, which the XO and Sugar are meant to enable, and he felt that the fifth-grade class would make an ideal test site for the potential of the technology:

> We focused on the 5th grade for a number of reasons. The devices seemed perfect for elementary students, and also fit in well with the elementary educational model, whereby students are with the same teacher for the bulk of the school day. We had hoped that skills developed would transfer well into other areas, and that the teachers' and students' investment would have large returns.[6]

Funding for the program was provided through a joint venture between a local educational foundation, the Parent Teacher Association at Van Cortland Middle School, and the school district. Through the pilot, all students were provided with XO laptops, and their teachers were taken through detailed training on how to use the XOs in general and how to incorporate the laptops into their classroom teaching. Suggestions were provided about how to use Sugar software to create "a series of curricular activities and projects" to engage the students in exploratory learning.

One innovation that emerged in the Croton-on-Hudson deployment was the creation of "Tech Teams"—groups of four to five students in each classroom were trained and empowered to be the class experts on the XO laptop and Sugar software.

> During this study, students demonstrated independence as learners in their classrooms during sessions where they used XO Laptops and their Sugar software. This independence was evidenced by what the teachers began to refer to as the "Ripple," where students naturally and spontaneously began to move to one another to work together and to share what they had learned to do on the XO Laptops. Additionally, when the helping interactions between students and teachers and those between students and teachers were quantified, students engaged in five times as many helping interactions between one another as they did with their teachers.[7]

Ardito incorporated these innovations into subsequent work he did with three Navajo elementary schools in and around Gallup, New Mexico, with an elementary school in Harlem, and with a program in Fargo, North Dakota.

In a 2009 presentation to the New York Society for Computers and Technology in Education, Ardito observed that the XO and the accompanying training have altered the "classroom ecology" so that now, "everyone is a teacher, everyone is a learner." Both students and teachers are recognizing that "making stuff is more powerful than just receiving stuff," and are relearning a new way to learn (and to teach) using technology—one that promotes greater independence and more creativity.[8] Ardito observed that the teachers designed curricular activities and projects in response to the changes in the learning environment induced by the presence of XO/Sugar. His results were significant in that they demonstrated not just development of skills by the students, but also a "re-formation of the classroom learning environment itself."

He also noted that there are some key challenges that the program continues to wrestle with: the right balance of use of the computers at school versus at home, how to resolve the need for wireless connectivity to maximize the potential of the computers, ensuring ongoing integration of Sugar's tools into the existing curriculum, and providing high-quality and sufficient student and teacher training. As you will see as you look across other case studies of OLPC deployments, these are familiar themes.

In a recent discussion with OLPC, Ardito observed that in the years since the two-year pilot, the Croton-on-Hudson deployment has evolved. Some teachers have continued to use the XO laptops, while others have discontinued their use. The XOs do not integrate well with the school's local wireless network, which has been a significant impediment in their ongoing use. At the time of the writing of this book, the XOs are primarily used to teach computer programming and robotics to Van Cortland students. As Ardito observed, "this has a great deal of potential and is something that will continue into the future."

LEARNING FROM THE COMPARISON

In comparing Birmingham and Croton-on-Hudson, it quickly becomes clear that there are a number of contextual factors—external to the school—that influenced the comparative success of the programs, as well as a number of variables in how the XO/Sugar was introduced to the school ecology.

- Unlike Birmingham, Croton-on-Hudson has had a consistent—and credible—champion for the project from the beginning who has been instrumental in garnering school and community support for the project. Importantly, as an educator, Ardito is able to connect the XO/Sugar directly to a vision of how it will drive teaching and learning.

- Croton-on-Hudson, being teacher driven from the start, has had a level of community engagement that is the hallmark of a successful deployment. Langford, in comparison, disempowered the schools and districts by foisting the XO on them as a fait accompli. Although the libraries and churches stepped forward to provide a venue for children to use the XOs, the effort became disconnected from the formal educational system to such an extent that it lost its power and credibility.

- With the top-down model used in Birmingham, the teachers were expected to use the XO to help students learn without support for their own learning about the use of technology. In Croton-on-Hudson, Ardito established a participatory model in which there was an expectation that both students *and teachers* would learn.

LOOKING AHEAD

In January 2012, five hundred students at the Holmes Elementary School in the Liberty City section of Miami received laptops from OLPC.[9] The project was funded by the Knight Foundation, which joined forces with OLPC in a digital literacy effort. Along with XO laptops, OLPC is providing "in-house training at the school for parents, teachers, and students on how to use the computers to advance students' learning." The closely monitored program has had sufficient impact on the children and teachers at Holmes that it is being expanded to all the elementary schools in Liberty City. A similar program is currently being launched in Charlotte, North Carolina, schools as well. After some false starts, OLPC may finally be gaining traction in the United States.

APPENDIX D

A VISION FOR THE FUTURE

OLPC IN RWANDA

"Our goal is to continue finding means and ways to provide all primary school children in Rwanda with this important learning tool. We are going to turn the dream of all our children owning computers into reality—it is possible to achieve this."

—Paul Kagame, president of Rwanda

IN RWANDA—A SMALL, LANDLOCKED, DENSELY POPULATED country nestled between Congo and Tanzania in Central Africa—a long history of ethnic tensions came to a head in April 1994. The trigger event was the deaths of then Rwandan president Juvénal Habyarimana and Burundian president Cyprien Ntaryamira, as the plane carrying them into the airport at Kigali (the capital of Rwanda) was destroyed by a surface-to-air missile. The killing ignited an already tense populace, and in the aftermath—over the span of only 100 days—more than 800,000 citizens were killed, primarily those from the minority Tutsi tribe killed by members of the majority Hutu tribe. Paul Kagame, then leader of the Rwandan Patriotic Front (RPF), which had been fighting the incumbent Rwandan government with US support, emerged as a military hero when he successfully toppled the government and brought an end to the genocide. After a brief role as vice president, he became president of Rwanda in 2000 and has remained in power since.

Kagame is a strong leader of a small country; he is deeply aware of the challenges that Rwanda faces and is intimately engaged in the details of overcoming these challenges to put Rwanda on a path toward development. Kagame has been effective in coordinating a coalition of affluent expatriates and a massive supply of foreign aid and technical assistance to support a plan for rapidly modernizing the country and improving the prosperity of Rwandan citizens. This plan, issued by the Ministry of Finance and Economics, and known as "Vision 2020,"[1] paints a bold vision of a Rwanda that has fully transitioned from a country fueled by humanitarian assistance into a country with a stable economic engine capable of transforming Rwanda into a "middle-income country" with healthy, well-educated, prosperous citizens.[2]

A 2020 LOOK AT EDUCATION

Vision 2020 rests on multiple pillars of development, including evolution of the agricultural sector, promotion of private initiative and entrepreneurship, enhancement of infrastructure including roads, energy, water, and ICT (information and communications technology), and—most relevant for OLPC—comprehensive human-resources development through a focus on education, skills development, and health. Success for Vision 2020 is transformation of Rwanda into a knowledge-based economy.

To enable this transformation, education is a key priority for the government. At a basic level, it is seen as a powerful tool for enhancing the well-being of Rwandan citizens. Education can be a potentially unifying force that can lessen divisions in the country by promoting a greater understanding of the broader context in which most Rwandans live—a tool for nation building, as it were. Rwanda is known as the land of a thousand hills, and in the past, rural Rwandans born into a small village on one of these hills were likely to live their entire lives within a few miles of their birthplace. The locus of loyalty and focus, then, gravitated naturally to the village and tribe; when exacerbated, the result was the tragedy of 1994.

In 2003, President Kagame made universal basic education—both primary and secondary—a major priority. The year 2009 saw the introduction of Rwanda's Nine Year Basic Education Programme (9YBE), which offers six years of primary and three years of secondary education to all Rwandan children free of charge. The impact has been immediate and positive: as of 2010, primary school enrollment was 97 percent for males and 98 percent for females, and secondary school enrollment was 92 percent overall.[3] While this indicates success in the beachhead effort to improve education in Rwanda beginning with primary school enrollment, these numbers mask substantial challenges regarding both the quality of the education and the retention of students into secondary school. From 2005 to 2009, only 31 percent of primary-school students were completing primary school and only 5 percent of students were attending secondary school.[4] While the elimination of school fees is driving increased numbers of primary completion and secondary attendance, the quality of the education and the ability of students and parents to justify the opportunity cost of time spent in school are critical to increased student engagement and attendance.

LEAPFROGGING AHEAD USING ICT

Rwanda has long embraced the potential of ICT (information and communications technology) as a powerful force to achieve social and economic development goals. In 1994, Rwanda had one of the lowest levels of penetration of electricity and telephone systems in the world; very few people had access to reliable power or communications, and the projected cost to build out the traditional physical network infrastructure was overwhelming. Cellular telephone technology proved to be the answer for Rwanda; the absolute cost of providing broad coverage was less than building a traditional, wired network, and the costs of doing so could also be distributed over time in a manner that made it feasible to achieve. This "leapfrogging" of older, traditional telephone poles and copper phone lines in favor of cell towers and microwave links achieved broad communications coverage quickly and cost-effectively. Just as importantly, it also proved to Kagame and the rest of Rwanda that a forward-looking approach to utilizing technology could help Rwanda not only recover from its past, but also truly prosper.

Building on this history, in 2000 Rwanda developed a National ICT strategy as part of their Vision 2020, an approach for investing in the physical infrastructure in Rwanda, as well as education and training of Rwandan citizens. It is against this backdrop that Kagame sent an invitation to Nicholas Negroponte and Khaled Hassounah, OLPC's regional director for the Middle East and Africa, to visit Kigali in early 2007. The minister of education, Dr. Jeanne d'Arc Mujawamariya and her associate, the state minister for primary and secondary education, Joseph Murekeraho, met the OLPC team the following day to discuss integration of the laptops into the school curriculum. The day ended with a state dinner hosted by President Kagame; in a bold pronouncement, Kagame committed to providing laptops to all Rwandan primary-school students (slightly more than 2 million in total) in the three years following the meeting. Although it subsequently took almost two years, in October 2008, Rwanda became the first African country to formally launch an OLPC project.

THE FIRST $100 LAPTOP

In the wake of the handshake agreement, the price of the laptops was a key barrier to be overcome in signing a contract with the Rwandan government. Kagame has a track record of negotiating very hard with donors to ensure that the Rwandan government retains a strong degree of control and that programs maximize impact (particularly hard to do in a situation where donor spending vastly outstrips the government budget). Kagame had become a public advocate of a new model for foreign aid that helped recipients become, to the degree possible, self-sufficient.

They treated OLPC no differently than other donors, pushing hard for the price of the XOs to remain at the promised $100 price point (rather than the actual price of $188). Since the size of the contract was large and the country was willing to move quickly, they felt they were on stable ground; what they did not know, however, was how little flexibility OLPC had to move given the constraints of its supply chain partners and organizational overhead needs.

The bridge between OLPC's cost and the $100 price point came from the Give One, Get One program to be launched in late 2007.[5] In late September 2007, Negroponte and Kagame met in New York and announced that Rwanda would be a recipient of an additional Give One, Get One machines for every machine they purchased directly—effectively halving the price of the computers. This brought the unit costs of Rwandan machines to $100 and marked the first time an XO was sold at a price close to the promised price point. The Rwandan government committed to the purchase and distribution of 500,000 computers in five years' time.

THE LAUNCH OF OLPC RWANDA

It took over a year to deliver the first XOs into the hands of children in Rwanda; the details of finalizing contract terms, arranging the letter of credit and preparing in-country partners to receive, store, and distribute the computers all took significant time to complete. Such was the dedication of OLPC and the Rwandan government to making the program successful that the OLPC Learning Team that was based in Cambridge, Massachusetts, and led by David Cavallo, relocated to Kigali in June 2009 to provide technical assistance and additional support for the project. The team setup the first (and, to date, only) in-country headquarters for OLPC. The main focus of OLPC Rwanda is to support the Ministry of Education's efforts to run the project.

In May 2009, Rwanda purchased its first shipment of 100,000 computers,[6] which would be deployed to 17 percent of their total target student population with a goal of eventually serving all students in the third through fifth grades. The laptops were to be deployed in urban and rural schools in more than 150 locations, and supports were to be put in place to ensure that the XOs were used in a way that supported the government's educational goals.

Providing needed infrastructure: Prior to deployment of the laptops, all schools receiving XOs were upgraded to include electrical outlets and electric lighting in the classrooms; the OLPC project was integrated into a larger effort to improve school infrastructure.

Integration with a changed national curriculum: As part of the overall strategy for development, Rwanda has invested heavily in developing a new national curriculum for primary and secondary schools through the Rwanda Education Board and the National Curriculum Development Centre, both of which report to the Ministry of Education. The new curriculum de-emphasizes traditional liberal arts courses like sociology and psychology and reinforces the importance of the sciences and mathematics.

Focusing on teachers as enablers: To drive a shift in the culture of teaching and learning, teachers have to spend time at the National Curriculum Development Centre. In the first 150 school deployment sites, the headmaster and one teacher traveled to Kigali for one week of training prior to providing the XOs to the students. Forty percent of their training focused on learning to use the laptop, while the remaining 60 percent focused on the methodology of teaching the Rwandan curriculum with a computer. Employing a train-the-trainer model, these two representatives return home to teach other teachers in their school.

School and community training: When the laptops are handed out to students, OLPC Rwanda staff spend an additional five days at each school site. They work with the teachers and students for four days and provide one day of training to the community to ensure, as OLPC Rwanda's coordinator Nkubito Bakuramutsa explains, a general understanding of "why we're putting these laptops in the school, the impact it should have on the students and why it's important for Rwanda."[7]

Extending support to older students: Beyond OLPC's standard approach of getting laptops into the hands of young children, OLPC Rwanda has also explored the use of the XO to accelerate the learning of older children and to create a sustainable support ecosystem. For example, TEVSA RWANDA, an association of all technical and vocational schools in Rwanda, works with young adults (ages 15–18) outside of the normal school system and helps them develop specific manual skills.

LOOKING AHEAD

Rwanda has been called Africa's "biggest success story" in the last decade of social and economic development. It seems that, likewise, OLPC Rwanda stands a good chance of emerging as a stand-out relative to other country deployments to date. As of the end of 2011, Rwanda had deployed 60,000 of its original 100,000 laptops to school children across the country. It has scaled back the timing for reaching its target of 500,000 machines; the 500,000-in-five-years goals gave way to the reality that the systems, support, and classroom integration need to be working well before the program could further scale.

That being said, the introduction of the XO (or other ICT) into education represents a huge shift in the culture of teaching and learning in Rwanda, as it goes beyond a long-entrenched rote-memorization approach to learning. According to Bakuramutsa, OLPC Rwanda's coordinator:

> Inserting technology in school is a fundamental change to classic education. It's not just enabling books to be in a digital format—it's a really new way of learning. We don't want them to repeat just what's on the board. We want them to demonstrate that they've really understood the concept. It's called constructionism—learning by doing.[8]

As is so often the case early on in a social change initiative, it is the anecdotal stories of impact that make the strongest case for the potential of a program. Such is the case for Mars, a shy fifteen-year old student in the four-thousand-student coeducational Kagugu Primary School in Rwanda's capital of Kigali. She was abandoned by her parents after the Rwandan genocide when they left to live in a remote village in the countryside. When she began at Kagugu, she was still recovering from the shock. Mars was generally one of the quieter students in the class and spoke little English. In her first year at the school, however, Kagugu became one of the many schools across Rwanda to receive XO laptops due to a new partnership with OLPC.

Mars began participating in "XO Time," a weekly challenge in which students complete a variety of activities using their XO laptops. One particular challenge required students to draw their own names using a program called

Turtle Art, which allows children to make images while learning concepts of geometry and basic computer programming. Although it took her two days to complete this challenge, Mars did so and felt the incredible joy of accomplishing a difficult task. As each week passed with XO Time, this formerly shy girl became increasingly confident in her abilities and demonstrated that she could speak English better than any of her peers. In the next year, when a new set of students came to office hours to receive help on their "XO Time," Mars—who had once been a student—became the teacher. She spent time with each newcomer and taught them the same techniques that she had been taught just a few months before. Mars has now advanced to secondary school and is often heard saying, "School is too easy!"

APPENDIX E

THE POWER OF STARTING SMALL

OLPC IN NICARAGUA AND PARAGUAY

"In Latin America, it has been the tradition to make money in a country and then take it outside. We are taking money we have made abroad and putting it back into our country, taking the risk and investing in Nicaragua when many people were not willing."

—Roberto Zamora Llánes

OLPC'S ORIGINAL PLAN FOR REVOLUTIONIZING EDUCATION in the developing world required that countries commit to large-scale purchase of XO computers. The rationale for this was that small-scale "pilot" programs would fail on two fronts. First, they would fail to put in place sufficient technology to reach enough students to truly begin to shift the culture of teaching and learning in the ways that matter to OLPC. Just as important, "pilot" programs were likely to fail because they lacked the degree of foundational commitment to the approach to enable the project to weather the inevitable bumps in the road that would emerge.

As OLPC has evolved over time, we realized that we were wrong about the potential of small-scale deployments. In this case study, we compare the similarities and differences between smaller-scale projects that were launched in two countries—Nicaragua and Paraguay—and the lessons we might draw from their experiences.

NICARAGUA

It is hard to say no to Rodrigo Arboleda, the president of the OLPC Foundation. Raised in Colombia, and a Miami resident for thirty years, he is extraordinarily well-connected in the Miami-based Latin American community. He is unapologetic about telling his wealthy neighbors that it is time to give something back to their home countries, and his charity of choice is One Laptop per Child. One neighbor who didn't need convincing was Roberto Zamora Llánes, founder of Latin America Financial Services (Lafise—a financial services company that provides currency exchange and investment banking services throughout Central America) and head of Banco de Credito Centroamericano (widely regarded as Nicaragua's most technologically advanced bank).

Zamora and his wife, María Josefina Terán de Zamora, have given more than twenty-five thousand XOs to children in their native Nicaragua since 2010. They have also provided technical and logistical support, funded training for teachers, and, when necessary, ensured free Internet access in schools. Their efforts represent a first step toward addressing educational and economic disparity that is long-standing and strongly biased against Nicaragua's indigenous residents.

The Republic of Nicaragua is the largest country in Central America, with a population of almost 6 million people, 70 percent of whom are mestizo (an European-indigenous mixture). Nicaragua has widespread underemployment, one of the lowest per capita incomes in the Americas (the per capita GDP hovers around $US1,000), and a minimum wage that is among the lowest in the Americas; the indigenous population is consistently on the lowest rungs of the economic ladder.

Nicaragua's first public primary school opened in 1837, and nationally funded compulsory education has been the norm since the late nineteenth century. However, lack of infrastructure and trained teachers, especially in rural areas, has consistently hampered educational outreach. In the early 1980s, the Sandinista government enacted an ambitious and largely successful literacy campaign; using secondary school and university students as volunteers, they reduced the illiteracy rate from 50 percent of the population to less than 15 percent.

It is against this backdrop that María Josefina Terán de Zamora and Roberto Zamora Llánes have established an OLPC program. Their family foundation, Fundación Zamora Terán (FZT), has helped bring laptops to tens of thousands of children in Nicaragua since 2009. Created as an outgrowth of Lafise Bancentro group's corporate social responsibility program, FZT has focused on expanding the reach of the group's charitable projects: specifically, support for education in Nicaragua. "Education," Zamora explains, "is the key to preparing children with the information and values they need to be well-prepared and knowledgeable individuals capable of transforming the social and economic conditions of their families, their community, and their country."

Nicaraguans have made numerous contributions to the Sugar learning platform (especially relative to the number of students participating in the program). And thanks to the local energy and engagement, FZT has been able to address problems that are unique to their deployment. An interesting example is the need to develop a new approach to inventory tracking. Typically, the distribution of the laptops is monitored by cross-referencing to a list of the names of individual children; in the Miskito culture of Nicaragua, young children do not have names: FZT was able to invent its own local cross-referencing scheme to solve this seemingly mundane but important problem. FZT has also been innovative in teacher training: its "Replication as a Strategy for Sustainability" model uses a model of "quality circles" by identifying teachers with leadership characteristics and engaging them in intensive pedagogical and technical workshops. These teachers become mentors within their schools. Other deployments are now looking to FZT for ideas and procedures to adopt.

Over the course of the program, there has already been measurable impact on student behavior in the schools that have received laptops. The number of children re-enrolling year after year has increased by 50 percent (and the drop-out rate has therefore decreased). The number of children repeating grades has also gone down, perhaps a leading indicator of both greater student engagement and learning.

The Zamoras hope that, through their efforts, they will lead the way for the government to expand the program to every school and every child. Until that happens, they continue to reach into their own pockets and also to reach out to third parties to help sustain and extend the program. In 2009, the Dutch foundation OpenWijs.nl, inspired by the program, started an educational "e-twinning" project between El Rama, Nicaragua, and the city of Maastricht in the Netherlands. Dutch volunteers were sent to help train teachers in the use of XOs, and two primary schools in Maastricht began their own OLPC project that connected their classrooms with those in El Rama. In another example of partnering, the Norwegian Fund for Investment in Developing Countries provided laptops to the children and teachers in the San Martín School of Rivas. In just two years, they have reached 25,000 children and, as this book is being written, another 15,000 laptops are heading to Managua. Perhaps more important than quantity is the quality of their deployment: the children are thriving.

PARAGUAY

With a population of 6 million, Paraguay is similar in size to Nicaragua. Unlike Nicaragua, the aggregate literacy rate in Paraguay is fairly high, with an
estimated 90 percent of citizens able to read, and an estimated 90 percent
completing fifth grade. The population of indigenous Guarani, however, face
challenges of social and economic inequality similar to those of the Miskito in
Nicaragua.

The OLPC program in Paraguay was initiated by an NGO, Paraguay
Educa, created explicitly for the purpose of introducing one-on-one computing to the nation's schools. Led by Cecilia Rodriguez Alcalá, the foundation
is independent of any commercial or government ties—although they have
secured some private-sector funding and, more recently, some government
funding from PTI Paraguay, the Itapu Technological Park, which focuses on
technology-based economic development. The Paraguay Educa initiative really took off when they convinced the OLPC Foundation to provide them with
four thousand laptops donated by the SWIFT consortium—a global, member-
owned financial cooperative comprised of more than 9,700 banking organizations, securities institutions, and corporate customers in 209 countries. (In
2007, SWIFT targeted OLPC as one of the not-for-profit organizations it supports as part of its corporate social responsibility initiatives; their donations
enabled us to seed initiatives such as Paraguay Educa with laptops.)

Alan Kay once defined technology as "anything invented after you were
born." Alcalá and her colleagues at Paraguay Educa—most of whom were less
than thirty years old when they started, and for whom using a computer is
more natural than pen and paper—didn't have to think twice about the benefits of putting computers into the hands of children. Their pedagogical team,
under the direction of Pacita Peña, had a further insight: the computer could
not only be helpful to the children, it could offer insights into the learning
mind. In Paraguay, OLPC was not to be just a replacement for textbooks. It
would, as the original vision of Papert and OLPC had emphasized, finally start
out being viewed as "a thing to think with."

The initial deployment in Paraguay focused on ten schools in Caacupé,
a small town located one hour to the east of the capital of Asunción. Thanks
to partnerships with the local government and national telecommunications
companies, Internet and electrical infrastructure was installed in all of the
schools prior to the arrival of the XOs.

From the beginning, they put an emphasis on building partnerships,
building a strong technical team, and building a strong pedagogical team—in
each case out-sized for the immediate needs of their initial deployment. This

has put them in a position where not only are they well poised to scale, but their program has also become a reference point for all other OLPC programs. As an illustration, one of their partners, the Paraguayan national media company ABC, runs an occasional two-page spread in the national newspaper focused on the use of Sugar activities; they began doing so when the project was still a pilot confined to Caacupé. Their goal was to build an understanding of and interest in OLPC ahead of the actual roll-out of laptops.

The technical team, under the leadership of Raúl Gutiérrez Segalés and Bernardo Innocenti, developed critical software components—such as inventory control—that are now being used by OLPC deployments globally in such diverse locations as from Peru and Rwanda. The customized version of Sugar that the team developed is used in Uruguay and Australia and is the basis of an international commercial spin-off. Peña has also set a standard of excellence through her ongoing insistence that the focus be on the learning, not the laptops. Her team has worked with the Inter-American Development Bank (IADB) to implement a baseline assessment strategy for use of computers for learning. They have also innovated new approaches, including the use of "*formadores*"—classroom mentors—and Saturday programming clubs to amplify the informal time spent with the laptops. And they have embarked upon a program to translate the Sugar interface into Paraguayan Guaraní, the first language of the have-nots in Paraguay. All these innovations have been picked up by deployments in other countries. It is not happenstance that the winner of a recent Nickelodeon programming contest was from Paraguay.

Another key to the success of the Paraguay project has been a focus on community. On a visit to Caacupé, at one of the schools we happened upon a standing-room-only workshop attended by parents who wanted to learn about the Sugar Journal in order to be better acquainted with the children's progress—unprecedented parental involvement in their children's learning. Under Peña's leadership, the program has encouraged students to have a more active role in the classroom by taking part in discussions, problem solving, or explaining concepts to other classmates who may be having difficulty understanding. As Peña explains, "The role of students and teachers are changing; the student becomes the protagonist of his own learning process, and the teacher becomes a mentor, a guide."[1]

In 2011, the project in Paraguay began to expand to three additional regions of the country; for 2012, OLPC will be assisting in the construction of a Digital Culture Center in Caacupé to which teachers from around the country can come to learn how to use laptops for learning. The Center will prioritize education, health, and skills related to creativity and entrepreneurship.

LEARNING FROM NICARAGUA AND PARAGUAY

When the OLPC model of sales of at least one million laptops gave way to smaller volumes sold to government buyers, the door was opened for non-government organizations and individuals to participate. These efforts generally start smaller scale but, as the experiences of Nicaragua and Paraguay illustrate, have the potential to be no less impactful in proving the potential of technology to improve education.

Importantly, these initiatives also tend to be privately funded rather than backed by government funds. This funding backdrop tends to create three key differences in the experience of the developments. First, privately funded efforts have tended to use a bottom-up approach that begins with community engagement, rather than a top-down approach of integrating first with a national education curriculum. Second, these initiatives are more likely to decouple measurement of impact from a strict focus on school performance metrics; the result is often great space created for innovation. Finally, these initiatives tend to attract greater support from international partners who can bring needed resources and support innovation and sustainability. While the classroom remains a critical platform for the application of the XO laptop and Sugar to enhancing learning, privately funded initiatives such as FZT and Paraguay Educa have been able to focus more directly on learning, rather than the educational system, and in so doing have provided leadership that is often lacking in government. In partnership with government, OLPC projects of this nature may provide a new map for how to impact at scale.

NOTES

THE VIEW FROM THE INSIDE: IN THE WORDS OF WALTER BENDER AND CHARLES KANE

1. Seymour Papert. *The Children's Machine: Rethinking School in the Age of the Computer* (New York: Basic Books, 1993).
2. Epistemology is a branch of philosophy that investigates the origin, nature, methods, and limits of human knowledge. In other words, epistemology explores how humans come to know and understand.
3. Alan Kay's 1983 *Scientific American* article on Agents discusses Walter's *NewsPeek* project. Mark Kortegaas 1994 MIT Thesis.
4. Alan and Michelle Shaw, Michelle Evard, Silver Stringers, Junior Journal, David Cavallo: Models of Growth, et al.
5. Marvin Minsky, *The Emotion Machine* (New York: Simon & Schuster, 2005).
6. Antonio Battro, "The Teaching Brain," in *Mind, Brain, and Education* 4, issue 1 (March 2010).

CHAPTER 1: INTRODUCTION

1. "Global Education and the Developing World" (The Peterson Lecture by His Highness the Aga Khan to the Annual Meeting of the International Baccalaureate, marking its 40th Anniversary. Atlanta, Georgia, April 18, 2008).
2. Adam Smith, *An Inquiry into the Nature and Causes of the Wealth of Nations*, ed. Edwin Cannan, 5th ed. (London: Methuen, 1904), 1.
3. Daniel P. Keating and Clyde Hertzman, eds., *Developmental Health and the Wealth of Nations* (New York: Guilford Press, 1999).
4. M. L. De Volder and W. Lens, "Academic Achievement and Future Time Perspective as a Cognitive-Motivational Concept," *Journal of Personality and Social Psychology* 42, no. 3 (1981): 566–571.
5. Stephanie Strom. "Nonprofits Review Technology Failures," *New York Times*, August 16, 2010. Accessed April 8, 2012, http://www.nytimes.com/2010/08/17/technology/17fail.html
6. Katherine Fulton and Greg Dees, "The Past, Present and Future of Social Entrepreneurship: A Conversation with Greg Dees," pre-reading developed for the 2006 Gathering of Leaders, Mohonk, NY. Published by the Center for the Advancement of Social Entrepreneurship, Duke University, p. 2, http://www.caseatduke.org/documents/deesinterview.pdf.

CHAPTER 2: THE ORIGINS OF ONE LAPTOP PER CHILD

1. "What If Every Child Had A Laptop?," *60 Minutes,* CBS, May 20, 2007.

2. Molly Lopez, "His Big Idea: A Laptop for Every Poor Child in the World," *People* 68, no. 20 (November 12, 2007).

3. "Nicholas Negroponte on One Laptop per Child," TED video, 17:41, February 2006, http://www.ted.com/talks/nicholas_negroponte_on_one_laptop_per_child .html.

4. Alfie Kohn, "How Education Reform Traps Poor Children," *Education Week* 30 (May 16, 2011): 1–5.

5. The theory and education system of constructionism was developed by Papert, as a direct result of his work to evolve and apply the earlier works of John Dewey, Maria Montessori, Paulo Freire, Lev Vygotsky, and, particularly, Jean Piaget. The focus of much of the work of these theorists was to better understand how children learn and to develop tools to help them learn more effectively.

6. "Papert on Piaget," http://www.papert.org/articles/Papertonpiaget.html.

7. Seymour Papert, *Mindstorms: Children, Computers, and Powerful Ideas* (New York: Basic Books, 1980).

8. In addition to Papert, the cocreators of Logo were Wally Feurzeig, Daniel Bobrow, Richard Grant, and Cynthia Solomon.

9. The name is derived from the Greek *logos,* meaning "word," and is meant to underscore the contrast between this new programming language and most existing languages that processed only numbers. The goal with Logo was to create a "math playspace" in which kids could learn and experiment with mathematical concepts using words and sentences.

10. "What is Logo?," http://snuet.com/CML/C03/C03_02.html#1.%20What%20is% 20Logo?.

11. The earliest year-long school users of Logo were in 1968–69 at Muzzey Junior High School in Lexington, Massachusetts. The virtual and physical turtles were first used by fifth graders at the Bridge School in Lexington, Massachusetts in 1970–71.

12. "What is Logo?"

13. A basic teaching of Jean Piaget is that children go through stages of mental maturation as they age and gain experience. Linda Jones, when reflecting on Piaget's influence on Papert, refers to Piaget's stage of "concrete operational thought." This stage is characterized by thought that is logical when concretely embodied. In other words, children from about eight to fourteen years old can usually functional logically when the problem is of a type that can be worked out with objects. Papert asserts that the Logo Turtle provides a concrete embodiment of ideas previously known only through abstraction. Logo can teach problem solving, logical thinking, and constructive methods and allows children to interactively create and manipulate abstract mathematical processes.

14. "What is Logo?"

15. "M.I.T. Media Lab Epistemology and Learning Memo No. 2" (September 1990). Its content was based on a talk presented at *Children in an Information Age: Opportunities for Creativity, Innovation, and New Activities* (Sofia, Bulgaria, May 1987).

16. Gary Stager, "An Investigation of Constructionism in the Maine Youth Center" (PhD diss., University of Melbourne, 2007).

17. Erik W. Robelen, Sean Cavanagh, Jessica L. Tonn, Vaishali Honawar, et al., "State of the States," *Education Week* 24, no. 35 (May 5, 2005): 54.
18. "Nicholas Negroponte on One Laptop per Child."
19. Named after the Costa Rican intellectual and humanist from the 1880s, a period of revolution and renaissance in Costa Rica.
20. "MIT Digital Nations Prospectus," http://dn.media.mit.edu/DN%20prospectus %203-03%20v3-eng.pdf.
21. "OLPC: 5 Principles," http://wiki.laptop.org/go/OLPC:Five_principles.
22. Laptop.org.
23. Laptop.org.

CHAPTER 3: BUILDING THE $100 LAPTOP

1. "Nicholas Negroponte on One Laptop per Child," TED video, 17:41, February 2006, http://www.ted.com/talks/nicholas_negroponte_on_one_laptop_per_child.html.
2. Moore's Law is the prediction by Intel co-founder Gordon Moore that the number of transistors on a computer chip would double approximately every eighteen months. Moore made the statement in 1965 based on an assessment of the development of the integrated circuit from its invention in 1958. Moore's prediction has proved accurate for nearly fifty years and is now closely correlated to the general development of computer processing power.
3. Nicholas Negroponte, N. (2007, December). "Nicholas Negroponte on One Laptop per Child, Two Years On," TED video, 16:40, December 2007, http://www.ted .com/talks/nicholas_negroponte_on_one_laptop_per_child_two_years_on.html.
4. Nicholas Negroponte, as quoted in Wilson Rothman, "OLPC's Origins: US and Taiwan's Hardware Lovechild." *Gizmodo,* August 27, 2008. http://gizmodo .com/5042466/olpc-origins-us-and-taiwans-hardware-lovechild.
5. Liquid-crystal displays (LCDs) are the screens used in most flat-screen televisions, computer monitors, mobile phones, and video game systems.
6. Interview with Mark Foster, August 2010.
7. Walter Bender, "The Seven Secrets of the Media Lab," *BT Journal* 22(4) (2004).

CHAPTER 4: FUELING LEARNING WITH SUGAR

1. "Nicholas Negroponte on One Laptop per Child," TED video, 17:41, February 2006, http://www.ted.com/talks/nicholas_negroponte_on_one_laptop_per_child .html.
2. John Dewey, "My Pedagogic Creed," *School Journal* 54 (January 1897): 77–80.
3. David Kolb builds on the work of Kurt Lewin to describe a learning process that starts with concrete experience followed by personal reflection on that experience. For older students and adults, the cycle continues into abstract conceptualization and active experimentation. David A. Kolb, *Experiential Learning: Experience as the Source of Learning and Development* (Englewood Cliffs, NJ: Prentice Hall, 1984).
4. Evangeline Stefanakis, *Multiple Intelligences and Portfolios: A Window into the Learner's Mind* (Portsmouth, NH: Heinemann, 2002).
5. Rebecca Herold, *Managing an Information Security and Privacy Awareness and Training Program* (Boca Raton, FL: Auerbach, 2005), 101.
6. Cynthia Solomon, *Computer Environments for Children: A Reflection on Theories of Learning and Education* (Cambridge, MA: MIT Press, 1986).

7. Cavallo, D., "Technological Fluency and the Art of Motorcycle Maintenance: Emergent Design of Learning Environments," (PhD thesis, Massachusetts Institute of Technology [MIT] Media Lab 2000).

8. In supply-chain management, the term "upstream" means "closer to the point of production than to the point of sale." In software development, "upstream" takes on a slightly more nuanced meaning. Software that is "upstream" is used as building blocks for software that is farther "downstream." In the case of Sugar, the software that is immediately upstream from us is the Gnome toolkit, which we use to create the Sugar interface.

CHAPTER 5: SELLING THE GREEN BANANA

1. "Nicholas Negroponte on One Laptop per Child," TED video, 17:41, February 2006, http://www.ted.com/talks/nicholas_negroponte_on_one_laptop_per_child .html.

CHAPTER 6: FROM THE WAREHOUSE TO THE SCHOOLHOUSE

1. It is useful to make a distinction between distribution and deployment: distribution is physical preparation and delivery of the XO laptops into the hands of children, while deployment is ensuring that the supports are in place to use and derive value from the XOs.

2. Ivan Krstić, "Sic Transit Gloria Laptopi" May 13, 2008, http://radian.org/note book/page/12.

3. In addition to the *OLPC Deployment Guide,* over time we have created tools for deployments that help them to determine necessary staffing levels, projected costs, and inventory spare parts, among other things.

4. Cavallo cataloged the characteristics of fertile environments for growth. He indicated that there must be a number of fundamental things in place for positive change to occur: (1) appropriation and experimentation—people need to try out their own conceptions of the ideas in their own settings based upon their own priorities; (2) concrete exemplars—there is a need to experience real examples of the ideas; (3) community and communication, including peer-to-peer interchange of ideas, and explanations from practitioners at a variety of levels of expertise and experience; (4) feedback—when one experiments, one must not only see the results, but also get feedback from others; (5) debugging—one must get the chance to "make mistakes" and then use those to design and implement further work; (6) materials—one needs things to work with that facilitate the new paradigm rather than merely working with the tools of prior projects; (7) language—new paradigms re-appropriate old terms for new connotations, and even invent new terms to describe things in new ways; (8) bottoms-up change—large-scale growth comes from many little contributions that emerge from activities on the ground ; (9) time and continuity—major changes do not happen overnight, as there needs to be enough continuous time to experience and develop the ideas in their full complexity; (10) volition—people must want to do things; (11) hope and expectation—people must come to believe that improvement is desirable and possible.

5. Nicholas Negroponte, NetEvents Press Summit, December 2006.

CHAPTER 7: NEITHER MAGIC NOR FAST: ASSESSING THE IMPACT OF OLPC

1. Sunlen Miller, "Obama: 'Our Generation's Sputnik Moment Is Back,'" December 6, 2010, http://abcnews.go.com/blogs/politics/2010/12/obama-our-generations-sputnik-moment-is-back/, accessed April 8, 2012.
2. "Increasing Government Effectiveness through Rigorous Evidence about 'What Works,'" http://coalition4evidence.org/wordpress/.
3. An additional challenge is that data-collection approaches for evaluation vary significantly across deployments. Some data are captured via national exams in reading and arithmetic, while others involve additional intervention in the form of surveys or focus groups. The resulting data range from anecdotal to qualitative and, in some cases, rigorous quantitative data sets.
4. Chong, Alberto, "Computers in Schools: Why Governments Should Do Their Homework," in *Development Connections: Unveiling the Impact of New Information Technologies* (New York: Palgrave Macmillan, 2011).
5. Claudia Urrea and Walter Bender, 2011. "Making Learning Visible: An Updated Evaluation Framework for One Laptop per Child."
6. "Let me add something raw and home based . . . ," http://olpcoceania.blogspot.com/2011/05/let-me-add-something-raw-and-home-based.html, accessed May 15, 2011.
7. John Navarro, "The One Laptop per Child Initiative: A Framework for Latin America and the IDB," (Inter-American Development Bank, 2006). The IADB Study was a large-scale random trial conducted in 320 schools, two-thirds of which received XOs. The study compared the results between the "treatment group," which received the XOs, and the "control group," which did not. The focus was on estimating the program's impact on learning in mathematics, Spanish, and cognitive and non-cognitive skills and behaviors.
8. Julián P. Cristia et al., "Technology and Child Development: Evidence from the One Laptop per Child Program," IDB Working Paper Series, Inter-American Development Bank, February 2012.
9. Daniel A. Wagner, Bob Day, Tina James, Robert B. Kozma, Jonathan Miller, and Tim Unwin, "Monitoring and Evaluation of ICT in Education Projects: A Handbook for Developing Countries," InfoDEV, November 2005.
10. Frank Bajak, "Laptop Project Enlivens Peruvian Hamlet," *USA Today*, December 24, 2007, http://www.usatoday.com/tech/products/2007-12-24-3577922877_x.htm, accessed April 8, 2012.
11. Sameer Verma, head of OLPC Jamaica, e-mail message, March 28, 2012.
12. Translated from the Spanish by Jody Cornish.
13. Zehra Hirji, Barbara Barry, Robert Fadel, and Shannon Gavin, "Assessment Overview of One Laptop per Child Projects," OLPC Foundation, September 2010, p. 18.
14. Ibid.
15. Chong.
16. The importance of teacher technological fluency has been reinforced in the United States as well. In the OLPC Birmingham deployment, one observer noted "significant variation in the impact of teachers on XO laptop usage in the classroom. Having teachers who use the XO more frequently and are more skilled in this use is associated with greater use, diversity of use and more positive attitudes toward XO laptops by students." Assessment Overview of One Laptop per Child, OLPC Foundation Learning Group, 2010.

17. Chong.
18. Emma Näslund-Hadley, Scott Kipp, Jessica Cruz, Pablo Ibarrarán, and Gita Steiner-Khamsi, "OLPC Pre-Pilot Evaluation Report (Haiti), Inter-American Development Bank Education Division—SCL Working Paper #2," June 2009.
19. Tabaré Vázquez, "Digital Democracy," *Americas Quarterly: Connectivity and the Digital Divide* (Winter 2009).
20. Mark Warschauer and Morgan Ames, "Innovating for Development: Can One Laptop Per Child Save the World's Poor?," *Journal of International Affairs* 64, no. 1 (Fall/Winter 2010).
21. Henry M. Levin, "The Social Costs of Inadequate Education," Paper given at the First Columbia Teacher's College Symposium on Educational Equity, October 2005.

CHAPTER 8: OLPC NOW AND IN THE FUTURE

1. Khan Academy, http://www.khanacademy.org/, accessed March 22, 2012.
2. Richard P. Feynman, *Surely You're Joking, Mr. Feynman* (New York: W. W. Norton, 1997), Kindle edition.
3. Matt Ritchel, "A Silicon Valley School That Doesn't Compute," *New York Times*, October 23, 2011, http://www.nytimes.com/2011/10/23/technology/at-waldorf-school-in-silicon-valley-technology-can-wait.html?pagewanted=all, accessed March 22, 2011.
4. "e-Mentoring for Student Success (eMSS)," New Teacher Center, http://new-teachercenter.org/services/emss, accessed March 22, 2012.

CHAPTER 9: A CALL TO ACTION

1. "Computers Employed as Teaching Aids," *Reading* (PA) *Eagle*, February 4, 1971, 28, http://news.google.com/newspapers?id=8wUrAAAAIBAJ&sjid=HpgFAAAAIBAJ&pg=3260,1746468, accessed April 8, 2012.
2. George Kembel, "The Classroom In 2020," *Forbes*, April 8, 2010, http://www.forbes.com/2010/04/08/stanford-design-2020-technology-data-companies-10-education.html, accessed May 19, 2010. Of course, slow technology adoption in education cannot be blamed completely on the establishment; the dearth of effective software tools and models for curriculum integration reflects a broader market failure.
3. Karim R. Lakhani and Jill A. Panetta, "The Principles of Distributed Innovation," *Innovations: Technology, Governance, Globalization* 2, no. 3 (Summer 2007): 97.

APPENDIX A: CAMBODIA, A DECADE LATER

1. The name Cambodia PRIDE was originally created by Ellen Hoffman, former editor for the Media Lab.
2. "Type II" status is an IRS status designation. A Type II relationship is one in which an organization is "(i) operated, supervised, or controlled by one or more organizations described in paragraph (1) or (2), (ii) supervised or controlled in connection with one or more such organizations, or (iii) operated in connection with one or more such organizations," "Internal Revenue Code: Sec. 509.

Private Foundation Defined," Tax Almanac, http://www.taxalmanac.org/index
.php/Internal_Revenue_Code:Sec._509._Private_foundation_defined.
3. They solved the power problem in Reaksmy by putting in place solar power for
the primary school and, for the secondary school, using Chinese generators fueled by diesel paid for by PRIDE.
4. Interview by authors, Cambridge, MA, August 2011.
5. PRIDE provides students with access to safe drinking water, hand-washing facilities, and a vegetable garden to supplement their diets. They also have integrated
health classes into the curriculum. As Elaine explains, "it's not just XOs"—not just
a technology initiative—"it's a community program." In building up this unique
community approach, PRIDE has learned important lessons about the other
types of support needed to enable students to be learners.

APPENDIX B: DRIVING CHANGE FROM THE TOP: OLPC IN PERU AND URUGUAY

1. Oscar Becerra, oral presentation, May 2008 OLPC Country Workshop.
2. Frank Bajak, "Laptop Project Enlivens Peruvian Hamlet," *USA Today,* December
24, 2007, http://www.usatoday.com/tech/products/2007-12-24-3577922877_x
.htm, accessed April 8, 2012.
3. Rebecca Winthrop and Marshal S. Smith, "A New Face of Education: Bringing Technology into the Classroom in the Developing World," Brooke Shearer
Working Paper Series, Brookings Institute, January 2012, http://www.brookings
.edu/~/media/research/files/papers/2012/1/education%20technology%20win
throp/01_education_technology_shearer.
4. Rossana Patron, "When More Schooling Is Not Worth the Effort: Another Look
at the Dropout Decisions of Disadvantaged Students in Uruguay," Working Paper,
Departamento de Economía de la FCS, January 2011, www.fcs.edu.uy/archivos
/0511.pdf.
5. J. P. Hourcade, D. Beitler, F. Cormenzana, and P. Flores, "Early OLPC Experiences
in a Rural Uruguayan School," In Allison Druin (ed.), *Mobile Technology for Children: Designing for Interaction and Learning* (Boston: Morgan Kaufmann, 2009).
6. Ibid.
7. Ibid.
8. Christoph Derndorfer, "OLPC in Uruguay: Impressions of Plan Ceibal's Primary
School XO Laptop Saturation," https://edutechdebate.org/olpc-in-south-america/
olpc-in-uruguay-impressions-of-plan-ceibal/.
9. "OLPC Uruguay: Request for Ceibal Proposals Out!," OLPC News, July 11, 2007.
http://www.olpcnews.com/countries/uruguay/olpc_uruguay_ceibal_proposal
.html.

APPENDIX C: OLPC AMERICA

1. Bob Blalock, "Alabama's High-School Graduation Rate Nothing to Write Home
About," *Birmingham News,* April 2, 2009. http://blog.al.com/birmingham-news
-commentary/2009/04/alabamas_highschool_graduation.html.
2. "Public Education Finances 2008," US Census Bureau, http://www2.census.gov
/govs/school/08f33pub.pdf.

3. Shelia R. Cotton, Timothy M. Hale, Michael Howell Moroney, LaToya O'Neal, and Casey Borch, "Using Affordable Technology to Decrease Digital Inequality: Results from Birmingham's One Laptop Per Child XO Project," in *Information, Communication & Society* 14, no. 4 (2011).

4. Mark Warschauer, Sheila R. Cotten, Morgan G. Ames, "One Laptop per Child Birmingham: Case Study of a Radical Experiment," *International Journal of Learning and Media,* Spring 2011, Vol. 3, No. 2, Pages 61-76. http://www.mitpressjournals .org/doi/abs/10.1162/ijlm_a_00069.

5. In Birmingham, for better or for worse, the death blow to the project came when Mayor Langford was removed from office in 2009 after being convicted of federal corruption charges. His fellow champion of the OLPC program, John Katopodis, former City Council president, was removed at the same time for misappropriating funds from his charity, Computer Help for Kids. Because of the lack of a local champion for the project and continued resistance from local districts and teachers, the City Council cut funding for the project in 2010. Birmingham now has the dubious distinction of being located in the first county in the United States to go bankrupt under Chapter 9 of the federal bankruptcy code. OLPC Birmingham, it goes without saying, is finished.

6. Gerald Ardito, "The Shape of Disruption: XO Laptops in the Fifth Grade Classroom (Middle School Teacher and Doctoral Student)" (diss., Pace University 2010).

7. Ibid., 121–122.

8. Gerald Ardito, Stephen Jacobs, and Caroline Meeks, "Sugar in the Classroom," Nyscate 2009. http://www.slideshare.net/guestea582ca/sugar-in-the-classroom -nyscate-2009-2554114

9. "500 Plus Miami Elementary Students Receive Laptops, Training," *BusinessWire,* January 27, 2012. http://www.businesswire.com/news/home/20120127005399/en.

APPENDIX D: A VISION FOR THE FUTURE: OLPC IN RWANDA

1. Paul Kagame, "Rwanda Vision 2020," http://www.minecofin.gov.rw/webfm_send /1700.

2. For Vision 2020, "middle income" translates into per capita income of about US$900 per year (up from an average of US$220 in 2000).

3. Rwanda Ministry of Education, http://www.mineduc.gov.rw/spip.php?article27.

4. "Rwanda Statistics," UNICEF, http://www.unicef.org/infobycountry/rwanda _statistics.html.

5. By selling laptops to individuals in the United States at twice the price ($399 each), OLPC was able to stockpile more than 90,000 machines in early 2008 that could be deployed as they saw fit. Negroponte was adamant that these machines not be frittered away in small lots to entice potential buyers or to enable "pilot" projects by less than fully committed partners. Given these concerns, using the machines to jumpstart the Rwanda project made sense.

6. "120,000 XO Laptops Headed to OLPC Rwanda," OLPC News, May 12, 2009, http:// www.olpcnews.com/countries/rwanda/120000_xo_laptops_headed_to_ol.html.

7. Moses Gahigi, "Rwanda: One Laptop Per Child Pilot Project Evaluated," *New Times* (Rwanda), August 29, 2008.

8. Matthew Stein, "Rwanda: A Program That Goes beyond the Classroom," *The Independent* (Kampala), August 27, 2011.

APPENDIX E: THE POWER OF STARTING SMALL:
OLPC IN NICARAGUA AND PARAGUAY

1. "Paraguay Educa: Making a Difference in Paraguay One Community at a Time," http://eclass.resource.s3.amazonaws.com/lib_user_3077417/pdf/1326931467_Ar ticle_20-_20ParaguayEduca_20Sebastien.pdf.

INDEX